GROUPWARE

Series in Communication Technology and Society
Everett M. Rogers and Frederick Williams, Editors

Everett M. Rogers, Communication Technology: The New Media in Society (1986)

Frederick Williams, Ronald E. Rice, and Everett M. Rogers, Research Methods and the New Media (1988)

Robert Johansen, Groupware: Computer Support for Business Teams (1988)

GROUPWARE

Computer Support for Business Teams

ROBERT JOHANSEN

With Contributions By
Jeff Charles
Robert Mittman
Paul Saffo

THE FREE PRESS
A Division of Macmillan, Inc.
NEW YORK

Collier Macmillan Publishers
LONDON

The Free Press
A Division of Macmillan, Inc.
866 Third Avenue, New York, N.Y. 10022

Collier Macmillan Canada, Inc.

Printed in the United States of America

printing number

1 2 3 4 5 6 7 8 9 10

Library of Congress Cataloging-in-Publication Data

Johansen, Robert.
    Groupware: computer support for business teams / Robert Johansen;
    with contributions by Jeff Charles, Robert Mittman, Paul Saffo.
        p.   cm.—(Series in communication technology and society)
    ISBN 0-02-916491-5
    1. Work groups.   2. Business—Data processing.   3. Business—
Communication systems.   4. Information technology.   I. Title
II. Series.
HD616.J65 1988
658.4′036′028553–dc19   88-11199
                                                                              CIP

To
Doug Engelbart and Jacques Vallee,
two pioneers of groupware,
before it was called that . . .

Contents

CHAPTER 3.   CURRENT VENDOR APPROACHES
　　　　　　　TO GROUPWARE　　　　　　　　45

Parallel to user efforts, vendors are dabbling with products and services that have a groupware flavor. We discuss nine current product classes as possible foundations on which groupware products might be built: five are hot prospects; four are longshots.

CHAPTER 4.   THE CURRENT USER/VENDOR MIX:
　　　　　　　CLIMATE FOR GROUPWARE GROWTH?　67

The 17 user scenarios from Chapter 2 are compared to the 9 current vendor approaches to groupware. Not surprisingly, the connections are only beginning to be drawn. Each current class is discussed in terms of enabling and inhibiting factors in the move toward groupware. Looking beyond current activities, we then provide our judgments about forces for and against groupware, from both vendor and user points of view.

CHAPTER 5.   SOFTER SOFTWARE:
　　　　　　　THE GROUPWARE WILD CARD　　　　96

Softer software is easier software, but it is also—at its best—more powerful software. Due largely to spin-offs from artificial intelligence (AI), there are definite prospects for softer software that could greatly enhance the attractiveness of groupware products and services. In this chapter, we sift through the hype surrounding AI to explore potential groupware aids.

CHAPTER 6.   THE OUTLOOK FOR GROUPWARE　　114

Groupware must be delivered over some medium, and this chapter presents a set of scenarios exploring how such infrastructures might develop. Then, we present our best judgments regarding groupware winners and losers.

CHAPTER 7.   DOING IT RIGHT　　　　　　　132

If you want to proceed with groupware, what should you do? We introduce scenarios for effective groupware use, followed by suggested methods for generating your own success scenarios. Finally, we propose guidelines for groupware implementation.

APPENDIX A.   GROUPWARE LESSONS FROM
             THE TELECONFERENCING MARKET   151

In general, computer people working on new products tend to ignore history. In this case, the history of teleconferencing has much to offer regarding what groupware vendors and users are about to experience. We summarize that experience here, beginning from success stories, but emphasizing pitfalls to avoid.

APPENDIX B.   SILICON VALLEY SURPRISES   179

Silicon Valley makes its living from surprising people, and there is no reason to suspect that groupware will be any different from other areas of computer innovation. Although the main body of the book explores likely developments that could affect groupware, this section takes a more adventurous look. In each case, arguments for and against the occurrence of a surprise are offered. Our intent here is not to be comprehensive or predictive, but to prepare (as best one can) for groupware surprises that might come to pass.

Preface

ROBERT JOHANSEN

This book is written for people who work in teams, either by choice or by necessity. Although it is a book about computer support for teams, it is more about teams than it is about computers. The story of groupware is a story of the dynamics of creating and using specialized computer aids for business teams.

Teams are small, cohesive work groups that have a job to get done—often a big job on a tight deadline. Most of the teams we have studied are business teams in project-oriented industries. But teams exist in the nonbusiness world as well: hospitals, community groups, churches, political groups, and many others tend to work in teams. Teams offer a practical way to get things done. But, as anyone who has worked with groups of people can attest, teams often move slowly and painfully—in either the public or private sectors. We tend to flag these problems with words: *committees* are bureaucratic and slow, but *task forces* cut through the red tape. *Teams* is still a positive word for most people. But some pain is bound to occur when people work together with other people, whatever this process is called.

We think information technology has matured enough for computers to be able to help teams of nontechnical people work together more efficiently and effectively. This book is trying to help that process along.

Our conclusions are based on research at the Institute for the Future (IFTF) that has explored the use of computers to support teams and the emerging market for products that provide such support. IFTF is located at the northern edge of Silicon Valley in California. By Silicon Valley standards, we are old timers, having been in operation for over 20 years. Our role in life is to provide an independent view of longer-term futures. Not surprisingly, computers have been a focal point for our work. We have learned, however, that the technology itself is only one piece of a complex puzzle.

My own background is as a social scientist who has worked with both computer scientists and users of computers for more than 15 years. I was born about the same time as the modern computer, in 1945. I did not get well acquainted with a computer until 1970, when I was a doctoral student at Northwestern University. At that time, computers were just beginning to communicate directly with human beings, in what came to be called *real time*. Thus, just as I was getting to know computers, punchcards were giving way to keyboards. This coincidence had a profound effect on how I came to view computers.

I got my first full taste of computing at Northwestern's computer center. Located almost underground on the lakeside of the campus in Evanston, the center revolved around a then-giant Control Data Corporation 6400 encased in glass—a spinning, whirring mystery to my social scientist's eyes. Those who worked closely with "the machine" were part of a new priesthood, not unlike scholars at the gargoyled Garrett Theological Seminary that is curiously juxtaposed about 100 paces from the computer center. It was hard to get "hands-on" experience with computers in those days.

The world has changed, however. Although some insider/outsider tensions remain between computer people and users, developments like the personal computer (PC), video games, and computer-bungled bills have made computers seem a lot more down to earth. In businesses, computer use has moved out of the back room. Whereas computers used to be the exclusive domain of data-processing professionals, the PC has jammed open the door to the computer room. Computers have become far too important to leave up to a single department. Those data-processing departments that have resisted this evolution have become like mailrooms, performing only those mundane operations nobody else wants to do. The more progressive companies have computer-savvy people on the executive floor, sometimes as a chief information officer (CIO), sometimes disguised as normal executives. The latter approach is usually more effective.

The maturing of computer use means that the technology can now be applied effectively to more-demanding business needs. The needs of teams seem to be a natural attraction for near-future computer use.

The research that led to this book was supported by a group of large telecommunications vendors who are thinking about future products and services. Our emphasis, however, has been more on users than on vendors. What types of group communications and computer support will users need in the future? How can computers help to provide such team support?

Our research has included hundreds of interviews with users and prospective users, analyses of new products and industry trends, and interviews with expert observers. This book builds on the conclusions from this ongoing research at IFTF, with an emphasis on practical conclusions—including opportunities and pitfalls. Our goal is not an academic report of research results, but a user's guide to a potentially important new area.

We have noticed over the past 20 years that emerging information technologies are often very hard to spot in the early stages. Such technologies typically are not completely new, and the core technology itself may not be new at all. Often, a "new" technology is really a repackaged technology, one in which the technology is matched more directly to the needs of a group of prospective users. The take-off of the PC, for example, was fueled directly by the usefulness of spreadsheets. *Spreadsheet* is a term that people can understand and relate to; it allows people to accept the new and foreign idea of a PC. Such repackaging and promotion are important, because they give users and vendors a banner under which to rally during the formative stages of a new marketplace. If the market reaches maturity, the banner may become a household term (as PC has become), or it may come to be viewed as part of another related field. We feel that groupware will be important as a banner for the near future, but in the long run it is likely to become simply a standard feature of personal computing.

New information technologies typically are very hard to name. We used to worry about that fact, for most of the new technologies we study are difficult to name. Then, we realized we had encountered a characteristic of most emerging technologies—if a new technology is easy to name, it has probably already emerged.

Our overall conclusion: computer support for work teams is an area that is hard to name, it offers many promising options for repackaging proven technologies, and there are strong user needs.

GUIDE TO THE BOOK

Because groupware is still coming out of its shell, there are many opinions about how it might develop. Indeed, there are many different motivations for pursuing groupware. Given these differences, we have structured the book to begin with a broad picture of what is happening now. Chapter 1 introduces groupware and discusses some of its roots. We then move on to both user approaches to groupware (Chapter 2) and vendor approaches (Chapter 3). As always, users will have different motivations and incentives than vendors, and it is important to consider both perspectives. Chapter 4 explores the current lack of alignment between user and vendor views of groupware. In this chapter, we discuss both the enabling and the inhibiting factors in the move toward groupware. We conclude with two separate listings of overall forces for and against groupware growth, from both user and vendor points of view.

Chapter 5 introduces what we feel is the most important technological force for groupware: the emergence of softer software. In particular, we discuss techniques, concepts, and technologies that can make groupware both more useful and more accessible to everyday business users. This collection of forces, influenced strongly by developments in artificial intelligence, constitutes a major wild card that could spur the growth of groupware.

Chapter 6 presents the outlook for groupware. Several alternative scenarios are presented, with interpretations that cut across these views. Finally, we present our judgments regarding speed of growth and likely winners.

Chapter 7 is directed toward current or prospective groupware users who want to create their own futures. Based on experience, we create a set of user scenarios and draw specific guidelines.

Appendix A provides a bridge between current groupware activities and the climate for change in both user and vendor camps. In this section we take a careful look at a class of technologies that we feel is very much akin to groupware: teleconferencing. One clue to understanding new technologies is to look for similar technologies in which some experience has already been gained. Although such comparisons must be done cautiously, the computer industry is even more susceptible to the opposite problem: it has a remarkable tendency to ignore history and consequently to remake old mistakes.

We feel that experience with teleconferencing over the past ten years provides important clues regarding the introduction of groupware. *Teleconferencing* (another naming problem) is a generic term used for technologies that provide group communications through any electronic medium, such as audio, video, graphics, or text. Whereas teleconferencing provides basic communications support for teams, groupware provides computing support. The most important lessons about teleconferencing tend to involve how *not* to do things, but these are very important lessons to learn.

A direct overlap exists between teleconferencing and groupware in some cases, in which teleconferencing systems also provide computer support, or vice versa. For example, PC-based graphics systems already are used in conjunction with audio teleconferencing for training and remote design efforts. Computer conferencing—software designed for store-and-forward group communications through computers—can accurately be categorized as both groupware and teleconferencing. But teleconferencing as an industry (a small industry) is more developed in the areas that have not relied upon computer tools.

Appendix B introduces a set of possible surprises (that is, low-probability events) that could influence the development of groupware, should they occur.

This book grows directly from research done at IFTF over the last two years, particularly market research on group communications and computing products and services. Our clients for this work have given us permission to use proprietary research, and we have added new research done at IFTF in the public domain. Our conclusion, based on this research, is that groupware is an important new class of computing products and services.

We have emphasized practical information that can be used by either prospective users or vendors of groupware products or services. Our goal is to make business sense out of the emerging market for groupware.

Acknowledgments

This book grew out of a series of team efforts at the Institute for the Future (IFTF). The Outlook Project was the primary source of this work. It is an ongoing project, now in its fifth year, that explores new directions in group telecommunications and computing activities. The clients for this research have given us permission to publish project findings, and they form part of the core of this book. We are very appreciative of that support.

The Outlook Project is a joint venture of IFTF and TeleSpan (Altadena, California). In particular, Elliot Gold has been a major contributor to the ideas presented here. Although time constraints made it impossible for him to be a co-author, his contributions are evident throughout the book.

Other members of the Outlook Project team deserve special mention, including Barbara McNeal, Shirley Singletary, JoAnne Goldberg, and Alice Andersen. At IFTF we also had significant collegial input from others, including Roy Amara, Ian Morrison, Gregory Schmid, and Richard Adler. The production of the book was greatly aided by Patricia Rogow, Judy Buchan, Patricia Stern, and Kathryn Lenihan—all of whom were working with the additional burden of producing a book at a time when we were going through a change in word-processing environments at IFTF.

David Sibbet contributed greatly to both the ideas and graphics used in Chapter 2. David is both a graphic artist and a person whose excellent ideas have helped us to visualize some of the groupware concepts that are still in the process of reaching fruition.

In the spring of 1986, as part of my role as an Affiliate Research Fellow at the Center for Information Systems Research (CISR) at MIT, I co-chaired a meeting on the topic of computer-supported groups. Many of the ideas in this book can be traced back to that meeting. In particular, discussions with Christine Bullen, Tom Malone, Michael Scott Morton, and Jack Rockart of MIT were extremely helpful.

At Free Press, we were pleased to meet and work with Bob Wallace. Everett Rogers and Fred Williams, series editors for Free Press, completed the team of people who gave us enough guidance to get the book going and enough freedom to get it done.

I was responsible for planning, drafting, and finalizing all the chapters. The three contributing authors (Robert Mittman, Paul Saffo, and Jeff Charles) were involved in the IFTF research that preceded this book, and all aided it greatly.

Robin B. Johansen played a critical role in envisioning and giving life to this book. Her enthusiastic support included provocative discussions, child-care relief, and much more. Our two little ones, Cory and Lisa, provided an important sense of perspective.

Our dedication is to Doug Engelbart and Jacques Vallee, both of whom are discussed in Chapter 1. Doug has had profound direct and indirect effects on all of us who are exploring the potentials of groupware. He also encouraged me to embark on this book as a way of pulling together the many vectors of groupware activity that are emerging. Jacques Vallee was my first colleague at IFTF in 1973, when we were evaluating the use of computer conferencing for communications among scientists. He was a mentor in suggesting ways in which my social science perspectives could contribute to emerging computer science applications. It was Jacques who said of the first electronic connections among groups, "It's nice that they were all linked together, but did they talk about anything useful?"

Robert Johansen
Menlo Park, California

CHAPTER 1

Introducing Groupware

ROBERT JOHANSEN

The personal computer is often *too* personal. In fact, much office work occurs in groups: teams, projects, meetings, committees, task forces, and so on. Group work is in fact a natural way of doing business and computers are just catching up to that fact. Now that many office workers have personal computers (PCs) on their desks, people are beginning to ask about connections to other people with whom they work closely. The personal computer is gradually becoming the interpersonal computer.

Groupware is a generic term for specialized computer aids that are designed for the use of collaborative work groups. Typically, these groups are small, project-oriented teams that have important tasks and tight deadlines. Groupware can involve software, hardware, services, and/or group process support. For example:

A paper manufacturer creates a groupware system to coordinate its manufacturing operation. Workers, supervisors, and management are linked, often across both distances and work shifts. The system allows more process control and improved coordination of individual efforts.

A group of managers has to reach a decision about whether to introduce a new product. A spreadsheet for text is used to identify key factors and weightings for each factor. The system supports the group decision-making process, which includes several face-to-face meetings.

A new catalog is being produced on a tight deadline, and input is needed from several company divisions. Group-writing software allows everyone to enter revisions and helps the manager to sort and prioritize each change. Text, graphics, and photographs are also included.

A brand team must respond quickly to a new advertising and promotional campaign by a competitor. Market data are retrieved

1

from external sources and analyzed and forwarded electronically among the team members, who explore and evaluate options and exchange statistical analyses, text messages, and graphic summaries.

A face-to-face meeting of managers is held with electronic flip charts. The purpose of the meeting is to generate a list of options the company might pursue in a new market. As the brainstormed ideas flow, they are typed into a PC and displayed for everyone to see. Connections and groupings of ideas are noted. At the conclusion of the meeting, everyone walks out with a printed copy of the ideas generated and the action steps agreed on.

Sometimes, groupware is used by permanent groups or departments. More often, computer-supported teams have a defined task (and often a defined lifetime) that shapes their work together. Group interactions may be formal or informal, spontaneous or planned, structured or unstructured.

Team members may be present in the same room, or they may communicate via electronic meetings in which all participants need not be in the same location. When electronic meetings are used, there are options for synchronous meetings (where everyone is present simultaneously) or asynchronous meetings (where group discussions are carried out over a period of time in a store-and-forward mode).

Computers are already being used by people on teams, but the emerging concept of groupware is different. Current computer systems that are used by groups of people (for example, time-sharing computing) are usually geared toward aggregations of individuals. That is, each user is seen by the system as a discrete unit or a point of input in a sequential process; there is little or no direct interaction, collaboration, or shared work among the users. Most of today's software and services are aimed at individual users and their needs. Groupware introduces a new dimension: flexible computer tools designed specifically for groups.

BACKGROUND

Although groupware is different from most of today's products, it is certainly not a completely new idea. Groupware had its origins in the 1960s and early 1970s. For example, in the early 1960s Douglas C. Engelbart created a laboratory at Stanford Research Institute (now SRI International) to explore the use of computers to augment the human intellect; he had a particular interest in high-performance teams. In the late 1960s, the Office of Emergency Preparedness was testing a computer-supported group system for responding to national crises, based on the Delphi technique for developing consensus among experts.[1] Rand Corporation was exploring the computerization of the Delphi technique to allow groups of experts to collaborate through an on-line network (Olaf Helmer and Norman Dalkey were the primary researchers in this effort). In the early 1970s the Institute for the Future (IFTF) was conducting field tests of computer-based conferencing for energy researchers, geologists, and NASA teams (the team at IFTF was headed by Jacques Vallee).[2] The New Jersey Institute of Technology began work in the mid-1970s on an experimental environment that would allow research on computer-support by groups (Murray Turoff moved from the Office of Emergency Preparedness to start this group).[3] These early efforts were provocative, but they have not had a very broad impact.

My own perspective on the field is shaped by working with Jacques Vallee at IFTF. This was an early exploration of group communications through computers, emphasizing collaboration among scientists. I was also influenced, directly and indirectly, by the work of Doug Engelbart, who is now at McDonnell Douglas. Engelbart is a little-known figure in most circles, in spite of the fact that he articulated and made a prototype of the first comprehensive vision of what *knowledge work* with computers might be like. Along the way, he invented the mouse, window-style screen displays, and other key concepts common in today's personal computing environments. Engelbart was also one of the first (perhaps even the first) pioneers of computer-supported teams.

When Engelbart talks of human augmentation, it is inherently team oriented. For example, he wrote this in 1963(!): "We do not speak of isolated clever tricks that help in particular situations. We refer to a way of life in an integrated domain where hunches, cut-and-try, intangibles, and the human 'feel for a situation' usefully coexist with powerful concepts, streamlined technology and notation, sophisticated methods, and high-powered electronic aids."[4]

In the early 1970s, Engelbart coined the term *augmented knowledge workshops,* building on the work done by Peter Drucker on the importance of knowledge work in U.S. society. Engelbart's focus was on the environment in which knowledge workers do their work, which Engelbart saw as a computer-supported environment, one with profound implications. In 1973 he wrote, "Workshop improve-

Douglas Engelbart's on-line conference room at Stanford Research Institute in 1967. This is the first such room that we know about and may be the first real example of groupware. Researchers shown are (left to right) Dave Hopper, Don Andrews, Bill English, Doug Engelbart, and Barry Wexler. Photo by J. Nipomnick. Photo courtesy of Doug Engelbart.

ment involves systematic change not only in the tools that help handle and transform the materials, but in the customs, conventions, skills, procedures, working methods, organizational roles, training, etc., by which the workers and their organizations harness their tools, their skills, and their knowledge."[5] Engelbart's augmented knowledge workshop laboratory developed early versions of concepts like collaborative dialogue, teleconferencing, recorded dialogue support, group writing, group programming, group databases, and multimedia communications. These are all concepts that are now beginning to appear in groupware products and services. Although Engelbart focuses on elite, high-performance teams, some of the principles can be applied much more broadly.

Engelbart's groundbreaking work provides a vision of the possibilities for computer-supported teams, but it also introduces the difficulties of making it happen. Engelbart began to write about his ideas in the early 1960s, but they are only now starting to happen. It is important to keep these periods of time in mind as we think about the future of groupware.

A new wave of research and interest in groupware has begun over the past few years. In the summer of 1984, for example, Irene Greif, then of MIT, and Paul Cashman of Digital Equipment Corporation,

Doug Engelbart at the console of the on-line conference room at Stanford Research Institute. A single console controlled the system, but each participant had a mouse that could be used during this meeting. Photo courtesy of Doug Engelbart.

organized the first meeting of researchers; about 40 researchers attended at Endicott House, MIT's retreat center. In the spring of 1986 the Sloan School of Management at MIT held a one-day workshop on the topic for corporate clients at its Center for Information Systems Research. In the fall of 1986 the first major research conference was held in Austin, and nearly 300 people attended, over half of whom were from industry research labs.[6] In the spring of 1987 the first user-oriented meeting on the topic was held at NYU's Graduate School of Business.[7] Research conferences on groupware and related topics abound. Meanwhile, groupware products have begun to occur with increasing frequency. Something is definitely happening.

THE TREND TOWARD BUSINESS TEAMS

Coincidentally with new technology trends, the U.S. business environment—including that of nonprofit organizations—is becoming increasingly team oriented. In fact, the concept of business teams is becoming popular quite independently from the trends toward groupware.

The participants in a business team typically are assigned on the basis of their ability to contribute, rather than because of a bureaucratic obligation. Thus, unusual combinations of people are usual within business teams. Business teams are cross-organizational, cross-divisional, or sometimes even cross-company. They are small in size (typically ten or fewer, but sometimes larger) and fast on their feet.

Examples of business teams include project teams, task forces, brand teams, sales teams, account teams, new-product teams, and crisis-response teams. The notion of a business team is not rigid by its very nature. It is a fluid organizational form geared toward an uncertain business environment.

Business teams are important to companies (as well as to nonprofit organizations) because they represent a way to organize for uncertainty.

Driving Forces

The trend toward business teams is being fueled by many developments. Consider the following driving forces, all of which are making business teams more attractive:

Industry deregulation. Industry deregulation in the domestic economy has created explosive changes for such industries as trucking, airlines, telecommunications, and financial services. This restructuring has meant that the organizational rules of the game have changed. In this climate of turbulence, business teams provide an immediate way to get things done without depending on old organizational structures or (necessarily) creating permanent new ones. The coordination and increased communication of the business team replace the command and control methods of management that, for heavily regulated industries, had not been used to dealing with competitive activities in a fast-paced marketplace.

Decreasing numbers of middle managers. Middle managers have been the key players in committee structures that have typified so many companies. Now, formal committees are giving way to informal business teams that perform in the same arenas middle managers used to dominate. Bureau of Labor statistics show that, between 1981 and 1986, almost 500,000 executive, administrative, and managerial workers lost jobs that they had held for at least three years.[8] The dwindling middle-management work force has left a vacuum that business teams often are being asked to fill.

A trend toward contract work. As the number of middle managers has decreased, many companies have increased their use of outside contractors to fill in gaps. The Conference Board estimates that the group of workers composed of part-time or self-employed people, temporary workers, and those who work at home has grown by 20% to 34.3 million people, almost one-third of the labor force.[9] Such contract workers give companies much more flexibility. Business teams can be important in such situations to manage and integrate the use of contract labor on an ad hoc basis. When the need is gone, the team disappears along with the contract labor.

Mergers and acquisitions. The trend toward mergers, acquisitions, and corporate restructuring has an effect similar to that of industry deregulation—there is a need for new organizational forms. Business teams provide a format for quick responses to the immediate demands (and threats) that precede and follow mergers and acquisitions. Although this trend is likely to be cyclical, there are plenty of current situations in which the need for business teams is very strong.

An increasing geographic spread for companies. Globalization is the extreme example of a trend toward increased geographic spread for business activities. Geographic spread implies organizations that cover great areas with great flexibility. Business teams provide such capabilities, particularly in the early stages of new organizational forms.

Team-oriented companies as models. Many of today's business success stories are stories of business teams, whether or not they are actually called that. Silicon Valley companies, for example, tend to follow the "Hollywood model" created for film-making: a team is assembled to create a new product, just as Hollywood organizes a new film. The team works together intensively until the product is out (in some sense of the word), at which point it breaks up and its members move on. This model of success continues to infect people with "entrepreneur's disease," and it creates an alluring image of success. Role models for business teams are also coming from more traditional business sectors than Silicon Valley. For example, John Smale (chief executive officer of Procter & Gamble) commented in the *Harvard Business Review:* "Our ability to reduce costs has clearly accelerated over the last few years as a result of the business teams approach. Another example is product development, taking a new product from the innovation stage—as we did with Duncan Hines cookies—and handling its execution as efficiently and productively as possible. The business team is a way of drawing on all the resources available within the company."[10]

Group-oriented performance ratings. One of the basic principles of Japanese style management is that performance measures ought to take account of the importance of teamwork. Rather than encouraging "dog eat dog," such approaches emphasize rewards for group performance rather than (or in addition to) individual performance. For example, Milton Pierce analyzed Japanese approaches to Japanese management and concluded: "A mistake by a team member is a mistake by all members. Success—and failure—are shared, and the team members must work together to correct errors. It may seem that this way of thinking goes a long way toward the destruction of individuality, but the 'sharing' philosophy also releases a great deal of pent-up energy that could interrupt the creative process."[11] As such performance appraisals gain popularity, people will be more willing to participate actively in business teams. Also, group productivity will often be easier to measure than the elusive notion of individual productivity.

Funding pressures on nonprofit organizations. In a climate of severe financial constraints on some hospitals, government agencies, churches, public-interest groups, and others in the nonprofit sector, there are strong pressures to come up with alternative organizational forms. Ad hoc teams can be used to develop responses in situations in which formal organizations no longer have any strength (for example, because of layoffs), or in situations in which an ad hoc group may be able to work more quickly or more creatively.

A tendency of nonprofit organizations to learn from businesses. One positive result of the gloomy funding picture for most nonprofit organizations is the new openness to adopting efficient and effective business practices. Many nonprofit groups can now relate to terms like business teams, because they have accepted that they must function like a business if they are to succeed in their higher goals (obviously, though the "function like a business" logic can be overdrawn in some cases).

The foregoing trends are not coming together in a simplistic problem equation that is solved by the creation of business teams. Rather, these trends are part of a complex maze of forces that will make the idea of business teams increasingly attractive to business and non-profit organizations.

Although business teams are becoming more popular, the business team approach provides no easy answers. There are important procedural issues to resolve, often including the most basic ones, such as who does what; however, business teams, because of their ad hoc nature and the importance of their tasks, often have more flexibility in how they conduct their business than do everyday business units. Also, they often have more money to spend, if money increases their chances of getting their jobs done on time. Business teams have a strong need to get a job done and an openness to new ways of doing so. They are ripe for innovations, one of which could be a form of computer support for teams.

THE DOWNSIDES OF GROUPWARE

As one thinks about groupware, it is important to consider not only its promises, but also its pitfalls. Although our conclusions lean toward the upsides of groupware, there also are potential downsides. For example, it is possible to have so many business team meetings that nobody gets any work done. Business teams can be overdone and employees are often asked to participate in them with no reduction in other responsibilities.

Groupware can also result in over control of individual participants. Just as the PC can be too personal, groupware can be dominated by the group or by a single point of view. There are real opportunities to exert social control within groupware systems, and it is easy to imagine how such control could be overdone. Groupware is not inherently democratic or authoritarian; it allows increased options in both directions. It is possible to design a groupware system that facilitates high individual participation in all decisions, but it is also possible to design group systems to channel people in a very manipulative fashion toward a particular direction. To varied degrees, groupware systems will embody beliefs about how people within a group ought to behave. The basic issue is this: Whose beliefs will be embodied?

More subtle than overt social control via groupware is the notion of "groupthink." The argument here is that groups implicitly can discourage dissent and bury individual viewpoints, even when such individual views are correct. Groupware systems will need to be designed with the risks of "groupthink" in mind to avoid such tendencies.

If groupware systems are *too* structured, they could also discourage creativity. This will be a delicate balance—how to achieve enough structure to encourage efficiency without providing so much structure that effectiveness is not discouraged.

Groupware systems are inherently less portable than personal systems. Somehow, groupware systems must allow people to work together, which often requires portability trade-offs. By portability, I mean the ability to move between systems with ease. Ideas developed within one system's environment ought to be portable to other environments. Groupware may encourage portability among group members at the expense of portability with people in other groups. Such trade-offs mean potential inefficiencies.

Finally, the increased popularity of groupware is certain to bring with it a parade of hucksters in pursuit of a fad to sell. Expect early examples of groupware grandiosity, hype, and overselling. In fact, such efforts, distasteful as they will be, may be an indicator that the success of groupware is actually beginning to occur.

Overall, the groupware downsides reflect concern more than they do reality. Concerns like this are important, however, and deserve careful consideration by prospective groupware users and vendors alike. This book takes a balanced view of groupware, although our overall conclusion is that the promises outweigh the pitfalls.

WHAT TO CALL IT?

As is typical of emerging technologies, naming is a problem. In these early stages, the prospectors of a new field try out various names in search of one that can capture the essence of a new idea and communicate it well to people who have never heard of it. As computer-supported teams have appeared in the past few years, numerous candidate names have appeared, including:

Computer-supported cooperative work (CSCW)

Technological support for work group collaboration

Workgroup computing

Collaborative computing

Interpersonal computing

Coordination technology

Decision conferences

Computer conferencing

Computer-supported groups (CSG)

Group decision support systems (GDSS)

Group process support systems

Computer-assisted communication (CAC)

Augmented knowledge workshops

Interfunctional coordination

Flexible interactive technologies for multiperson tasks

Though each of these names has its merits, they are not the sort of names that stir the hearts of prospective users.

I have heard the term groupware on several occasions over the past few years, beginning in the early 1980s. Cal Pava of the Harvard Business School used the term at about that time, as did Peter and Trudy Johnson-Lenz, who work over an electronic information network called EIES (New Jersey Institute of Technology). There were probably other early users of the groupware term and, as usual, it is very difficult to determine who really coined it. The first time I saw groupware in the mass-market press was in the *Fortune* article called "Software Catches the Team Spirit."[12] *Fortune's* use of the term groupware as a generic shorthand for group-oriented computer tools increases the chances that the term will catch on in wider circles. Aside from that, it provides a catchy word that is much more easy to use than most of the bulky phrases noted above.

Our only hesitancy about the term groupware is that it might be misinterpreted by some readers. The groups we are concentrating on are primarily small teams rather than large, formal organizations. Also, the "ware" needed is not simply hardware or even software; group process techniques are also very important. So, we have selected the term groupware as the best generic name seen to date, even though it does have some limitations. This book will try to create a comprehensive definition of groupware and where it might go. Groupware is a loose cluster of activities that involves computer support for teams of collaborators. It is a market that is not yet a market, a new communications medium still reaching for its final form.

CHAPTER 2

Current User Approaches
to Groupware

ROBERT JOHANSEN

A good rule of thumb in the exploration of emerging technologies is to start with the users, even if there are only a few of them around. This chapter is the result of discussions with such users, as well as other early pioneers of groupware. The goal here is to lay out a range of views regarding functions that groupware might perform for users.

APPROACHES TO COMPUTER-SUPPORTED TEAMS

What could groupware do to support the work of business teams? This chapter introduces 17 approaches to team support as it is already beginning to appear. A definite overlap occurs among some of the approaches, but each has its own perspective. These 17 approaches represent a variety of possible steps toward computer-supported teams; the steps get larger (with reference to the present) as the list progresses. Each approach is described, illustrated by a brief scenario, and followed by a brief assessment of the current status of this approach and a notation of possible pitfalls. We then come back to categorization of the scenarios. All 17 of these approaches are groupware by the definition given in Chapter 1, but they represent different angles on an emerging marketplace.

In a few of the scenarios, we mention companies or products that illustrate this approach to groupware. We have only included companies and products that we are relatively sure will last for the fore-

Note: The graphic illustrations in this chapter were done by David Sibbet, who has an extremely useful knack for visualizing the key elements of emerging technology concepts. We feel that the use of graphics to explore new technologies, particularly those that are difficult to name, will increase in importance in the near future.

seeable future, however. Not surprisingly, application of this rule of selection means that many current products did not get included.

1. Face-to-Face Meeting Facilitation Services

Face-to-face meetings are already a way of life in business, and there are people who specialize in facilitating these meetings. Typically, such facilitators work independently on a consulting basis, but large companies sometimes have in-house people who are on call to help make meetings work. Today, the normal tools of the facilitator are the flip-chart pad and the felt-tip pen. What if electronic support for the facilitator were available, which, in turn, could support the activities of a work team?

SCENARIO 1: CHAUFFEUR (SUPPORT FOR FACE-TO-FACE MEETINGS)

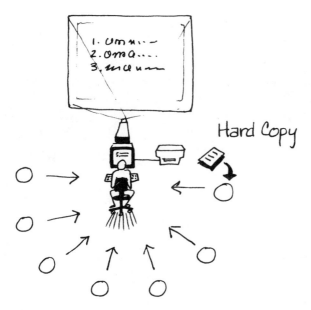

The team members are in a spirited argument as they explore their options for presenting an interim report on their work to date. This is a meeting to plan the presentation they have scheduled with their boss in two weeks, the halfway point in their task-force assignment. As the team members talk with each other, a facilitator types quietly

System developed by Meeting Technologies for facilitation of face-to-face meetings, an example of the "Chauffeur" scenario. Three Apple Macintosh computers are lashed together with special software for group recording and a large display screen that all participants can see. Photo courtesy of Meeting Technologies, Inc. (Berkeley, CA).

at the side, recording summary phrases from each statement that are projected on a screen for the group to see. Periodically, he stops the meeting and asks the group members to look at what he has recorded and to check it for accuracy; he then tries to organize what he is hearing into a more coherent whole. (If the facilitator does not understand, there is little chance that the boss would understand.) Some of the notes created by the facilitator look like electronic versions of what would have been written on flip-chart pads. There also are brainstormed lists of ideas and graphic summaries that the facilitator thinks might work for the executive presentation. As the meeting ends, the team agrees on four alternatives for consideration. Draft versions, along with the complete meeting notes, are printed on a laser printer at the back of the room and photocopied for the team members to take with them as they leave.

CURRENT STATUS: A small company called Meeting Technologies (Berkeley, California) performs a service quite similar to the one described in the scenario, using three Macintosh computers that they have connected together and some special software they have written for group recording. Several other group facilitation companies are moving in a similar direction. Also, several user organizations have constructed permanent rooms to support such facilitation activities.

POSSIBLE PITFALLS: Facilitators are not well accepted in most companies. In addition, most facilitators are not adept at computer use, and the software tools for such facilitation are not yet fully developed. Conference rooms will have to be specially equipped to support such activities, or the facilitators will have to carry their equipment—like traveling rock groups.

2. Group Decision Support Systems

Decision support systems (DSS) have gradually emerged and are used heavily within many user companies. Keen and Scott Morton introduced the concept of DSS as the use of computers to: "(1) assist managers in their decision processes in semi-structured tasks; (2) support, rather than replace, managerial judgment; (3) improve the effectiveness of decision making, rather than its efficiency."[1] Why not extend the DSS concept into group decision support systems (GDSS)?

SCENARIO 2: GDSS (SUPPORT FOR FACE-TO-FACE MEETINGS)

The team has to decide. There are seven different views among the seven team members, but they have to reach one decision. The first thing they agree upon, though not easily, is how to phrase the ques-

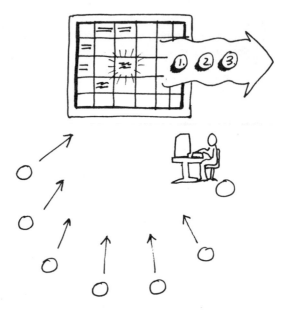

tion, how to decide what they have to decide. Next, the GDSS asks them for anonymous judgments, it asks them about their own uncertainties, and it asks them to self-rate their expertise. After all the team members have entered their judgments, the system does some aggregation of the opinions and feeds back a first-round set of judgments from the group. The group goes through a series of these "rounds" until a decision is reached. The system certainly does not make the decision, but it provides an effective and efficient group decision-making process.

CURRENT STATUS: GDSSs have been in use in limited ways for almost 20 years. Kraemer and King have conducted a recent survey of such systems and conclude that, in spite of years of attempts, "The field of GDSSs is as yet not well developed, even as a concept."[2] There are isolated examples, but there is little success to report. Research activities, however, are increasing, and the techniques for decision support are becoming both more powerful and less obtrusive for users.

POSSIBLE PITFALLS: Formal procedures for decision making often are frowned upon by "real business people"; significant changes in perceptions and procedures may need to occur. Decision support tools, although plentiful for individuals, often lack the flexibility needed for group applications in business.

One of the early examples of a commercial group decision support system (GDSS) is The Pod, by ICL in England. This system includes computer equipment, software, modular walls, a meeting table, display devices and other tools for what ICL refers to as "decision conferences." Photo courtesy of Robin Seward and International Computers Limited (Berkshire, England)

Conference rooms may need to be adapted to allow for GDSS, and this adaptation is likely to be expensive. Most companies are used to conference room expenditures that only include items like overhead and slide projectors, or (perhaps) a speakerphone—not expensive equipment.

3. Computer-Based Extensions of Telephony
for Use by Work Groups

The telephone is a workstation that is familiar to everyone. If it is possible to build from the telephone, the leap to computer-supported teams does not seem as great for prospective users. There are two basic approaches that could overlap. One builds on the capabilities of the telephone network itself (or private networks); the other builds on the on-premises private branch exchanges (PBXs) or the smaller systems, called keysets, that are already common and are becoming powerful.

SCENARIO 3: TELEPHONE EXTENSION
(SUPPORT FOR ELECTRONIC MEETINGS)

The team meeting is booked for 2:00 P.M., and the phones ring right on time. Each team member sits at his or her desk, hundreds of miles apart, with a screen display that shows a virtual conference room table indicating who is present and who is talking at the given time. All of the seven team members are acknowledged on the screen, with their voices coming through the high-quality loudspeaker telephone. When a team member has a draft or some data to show, it can also appear on the screens. To the team members, the system is an extension of their telephones, an extension that includes what they used to do on a PC and what they used to do through a surly conference-call operator. Face-to-face meetings still occur, but the telephone meetings provide the opportunity for much more regular communications.

CURRENT STATUS: Northern Telecom's Meridian already provides services very much like this scenario, including one called Meeting Communication Services. Meridian is a PBX (essentially, a private on-premise telephone system for medium to large companies) that also acts for all the world like a computer. From another perspective, a telephone-network-based product that provides capabilities similar to those in the scenario is the AT&T Alliance bridging service. This service now provides long-distance conference calling for much of the United States through a digital bridge that also has capabilities for exchanging graphics among group members. These are both leading-edge products, but we expect that they will be followed by an increasing number of group-oriented telephony products and services.

POSSIBLE PITFALLS: PBXs are just developing group support capabilities, and these capabilities may be tied to expensive purchases of complete new PBX systems. This linkage to larger systems is positive in the sense that group support capabilities will be positioned as features on the new system, but it also means that it may be difficult for teams to get access to such systems without becoming involved in a larger purchase decision. (Network-based services do not have this problem, because they can be sold as services and prices can be based on use.) Telephony-based approaches also need to be connected in some way to the computing equipment already used by teams, and this connection, in some cases, may be difficult. Also, even though digital conference calling bridges make it easy to hear all participants, many prospective users remember only the early days (not so long ago) of straining to hear who is saying what.

4. Presentation Support Software

Team members often have to make presentations, either to the team itself or to people who have an interest in what the team is doing. Software can make the process of preparing presentations much easier, even if the meetings themselves have no new electronic aids. Instead of relying only on a graphics artist, with frequent long delays, many presentations can be prepared by the author. Professional graphics assistance can also come into play, but many uses of graphics for teams do not require such specialized skills. Thus, the desktop becomes functionally linked to the podium. Each team member can use the system, rather than relying on a "chauffeur."

SCENARIO 4: PRESENTATION PREP
(SUPPORT FOR FACE-TO-FACE MEETINGS)

The team has worked over the ideas for weeks. Now it is time to do a briefing for the boss and the boss's boss. Vugraphs (overheads) are the medium of choice in this company, so the new ideas have to be boiled down into vugraphs. Each team member has played with vugraph content, formats, and styles before the meeting. After going through various drafts, the team finally agrees on just the right "look" for its presentation. Then comes the final rush: as usual, there are changes up to the last five minutes before the meeting. When it is over, the presentation looks great, except for the laser-printed typo in the lower-right-hand corner of the concluding paragraph.

CURRENT STATUS: Presentation software is becoming more common, primarily because of the rise of desktop publishing, in which high-quality laser printing can be done very easily and inexpensively. Indeed, presentation software is a variant of desktop publishing. One aerospace company has developed software that is geared toward its own internal project briefings, with slide-preparation software (for preparation and display on PCs) and links to conference calling capabilities. Several software companies are introducing extension packages that allow output from existing software (for example, a spreadsheet or idea processor) in a form that can be used directly for presentations.

POSSIBLE PITFALLS: Such software may introduce role conflicts within an organization: presenters are not used to creating their own visuals, and graphics artists may feel left out. Role changes will need to occur, such as presenters learning enough about style and format to use the software. Graphics artists will need to learn the software and adapt their skills to those areas in which a nonartist with software cannot perform well. In addition, quality-control problems can arise, resulting in what has been called ''laser crud.''

---

5. Project Management Software

Work teams have obvious and often pressing needs for task planning and coordination. Specialized software could help them plan what needs to be done, track their progress in reaching goals, and coordinate activities under way by individual team members. The big issue with project management software is to find a system that all team members will actually use.

SCENARIO 5: TEAM CONSCIENCE
(SUPPORT BETWEEN MEETINGS)

The team has better things to do with its time than keep records. There is a harsh set of deadlines to remember, however. While the team focuses on the content of its work, the system has a basic record of tasks to be conducted, task assignments, subtask breakdowns, and schedules. Each team member reviews his or her progress with the

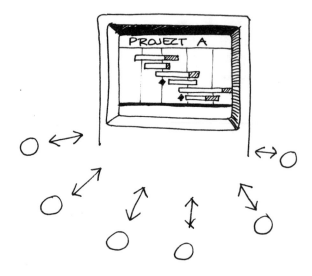

system on a weekly basis; the system is used during team meetings every other week. The software has very little intelligence; it simply organizes what the team has to do and reminds the members when it has to be done. Each face-to-face meeting of the team opens with a computer-aided review. This discipline and resulting coordination is probably more important than the actual functions performed by the software.

CURRENT STATUS: Project management software is becoming increasingly common in the PC arena and increasingly good as well. Some systems even include limited system intelligence that "remembers" the group's schedule and monitors its progress or lack of same.

POSSIBLE PITFALLS: Any approach to project management must be used by all key team members in order to be valuable. Project management software must be compatible enough with the styles of team members to allow this participation to occur. This will be tough for software designers, because the needs and styles of work teams will vary greatly.

---

6. Calendar Management for Groups

This is a straightforward approach: work teams need to coordinate calendars with each other and perhaps with others. Unfortunately, implementation is not as straightforward as the concept implies. Many people are reluctant to use computer-based calendars in the first place, often for good reason. Yet anyone who has tried to schedule a meeting among several busy people must have thought: there must be a better way.

SCENARIO 6: OUR BLACK BOOK (SUPPORT BETWEEN MEETINGS)

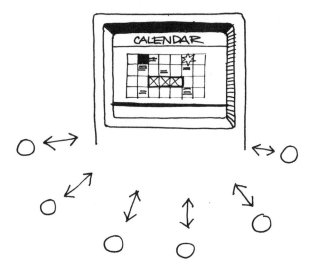

Each team member designates times that are unavailable and available, with a weighting that indicates flexibility in the event the system has trouble finding matches of free time. At first, it is hard to get everyone to use the system. Gradually, however, the team agrees that the black book should be the calendar of last resort and that each team member has to be responsible for keeping his or her own calendar in synch. "If only it would fit in my pocket!" is the recurrent lament. Meanwhile, the black book quietly records people's schedules and suggests the most promising meeting dates and times.

CURRENT STATUS: Electronic calendars have been accepted very slowly within most user communities, especially by those people who have secretaries or assistants who schedule meetings for them so they can avoid the hassle. Gradually, however, individual calendaring systems are coming into the marketplace. Group-oriented calendaring products are just beginning to appear in the market. On the research side, the logistics of group calendaring are becoming better understood, and applications are promising.[3]

POSSIBLE PITFALLS: As with project management, group calendaring requires full participation, and this will be difficult to achieve on many teams. In addition, many people are very protective of their personal calendars; these people are likely to resist the notion of an electronic calendar, especially when it is shared and—to some extent—under the control of others.

7. Group-Authoring Software

Group authorship is already a common practice, typically via a series of scrawled comments that are centralized onto one draft before changes are made. Group-authorship software allows team members to make document revisions, with the system remembering who made which changes. Team members can suggest changes without wiping out the original; comparisons among alternative drafts are easily made. The overall goal is to improve the speed and quality of group writing.

SCENARIO 7: GROUP WRITING (SUPPORT BETWEEN MEETINGS)

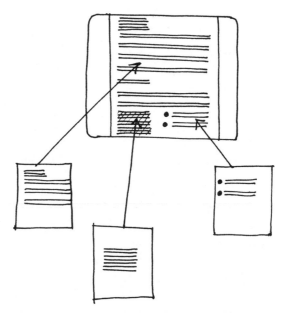

The brief is being filed today in San Francisco because that is where the court is, but the principal attorneys are in New York and Washington. The first draft was written in New York and transmitted electronically to Washington and San Francisco. Changes were made in all three cities; the system kept all the versions of the brief, with indications of authorship. The lead attorney made decisions to take one paragraph from Washington, another one from San Francisco, and so on. The brief is being filed on time.

CURRENT STATUS: Group-authoring software has been introduced recently by at least five separate companies, all with interesting products.[4] These introductions, however, have just occurred, and it is too early to see how successful they will be. Some word-processing programs also are being expanded to include group-writing capabilities.

POSSIBLE PITFALLS: Group writing is a delicate process at best, and working together through software could increase the difficulties for some work teams. This delicacy magnifies the problems inherent in creating group-writing software. Even if the software works well, coordination of the various authors will be critical to success. Some teams may give up early, because the barriers of behavior change, learning, and coordination are too imposing.

---

8. Computer-Supported Face-to-Face Meetings

In this case, the team members work directly with computers, rather than through a "chauffeur" (as in Scenario 1). This is a bigger step, of course. There is a requirement for more than one workstation in the room, for software that can provide direct group support, and for enough user skills to make it possible. It builds, however, on the familiar notion of face-to-face meetings. As Mark Stefik of Xerox Palo Alto Research Center (PARC), developer of the most advanced system of this type states, the primary competition is the white board.

SCENARIO 8: BEYOND THE WHITE BOARD (SUPPORT FOR FACE-TO-FACE MEETINGS)

Each team member had been working on a section of the final report. Members walk into the specially equipped room with diskettes in hand (although one person has managed to send his files through the company's local area network from his desktop workstation to the

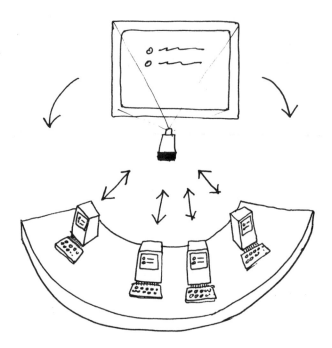

conference room). The half-circle table includes four PCs connected together and a display screen. Team members work privately during the meeting or display their work for others to see. In the meeting, they work through each section of the final report, doing revisions on the fly. When they leave the room, they leave with a common "group memory" of what has occurred and which next steps will occur next. They also have an impressive, jointly authored draft to build on.

CURRENT STATUS: The COLAB at Xerox PARC is already beyond this scenario, though only as an R&D activity. It is based in the Intelligent Systems Laboratory at PARC and is designed for a high-level team of artificial intelligence (AI) researchers.[5] Several commercial attempts to develop more limited systems have met with little commercial success.[6] Research experience, however, is yielding significant insights that can contribute to future products.

POSSIBLE PITFALLS: The technology for acting out this scenario is almost here, but it is difficult and expensive to assemble. Integration of the hardware components is also tricky, and the software, in most cases, is only available in advanced R&D settings. Once all the equipment is assembled and integrated, imposing issues remain in making such a system easy to use by most people. The issue mentioned in Scenario 2 regarding the

The COLAB at Xerox Palo Alto Research Center is an example of the "Beyond the Whiteboard" scenario. Participants have individual workstations, as well as a display screen. The lectern (referred to as the "electern") also contains a keyboard and mouse. Danny Bobrow, one of the creators of COLAB along with Mark Stefik, is shown at the electern. Photo courtesy of Xerox Corporation.

reluctance of companies to spend money on equipment for conference rooms is also a pitfall.

9. PC Screen-Sharing Software

If one person can make good use of a PC and that person is also involved in team efforts, would it not be useful for that person to be able to "share screens" with other team members? This approach to computer-supported teams builds directly on PC use: anything that can be displayed on a PC screen could be shared with another (and perhaps more than one other) PC screen. The result has been labeled by Xerox PARC as WYSIWIS (what you see is what I see), pronounced "wizeewiz."

SCENARIO 9: SCREEN SHARING
(SUPPORT FOR ELECTRONIC MEETINGS)

"I think we should move this circle over here and turn the arrow in this direction. . . . " He talks as he moves the circle and redraws the arrow on his PC, and the other team members see it change on their PCs as he does it. They are also connected by conference call to discuss the revisions. They are in a "scratchpad" region of the computer software program right now, but the system keeps track of the drafts and of who creates what. At the end of the meeting, everyone has a revised version on his or her own PC.

CURRENT STATUS: Various attempts to build PC software for screen sharing have been mounted over the past several years. Thus far, commercial success has come slowly, but there are definite signs of progress. There seem to be at least two problems: first, it is tricky for users to get the logistics down (to be sure the right diskette is in the right drive, the right modem settings, and so on). Second, although the idea of screen sharing is immediately attractive to many PC users, it also requires some behavior change. Screen-sharing software is a logical stepping-stone class of products. Screen sharing for specialzied teams, such as architects or engineers doing computer-assisted design (CAD), seems to be the most likely early applications area.

POSSIBLE PITFALLS: Screen sharing is one of those ideas that looks great in principle but that has sticky problems at the implementation stage.[7] As indicated, the logistics of multiple users and multiple screens can be very difficult for both systems designers and users.

---

10. Computer-Conferencing Systems

Computer conferencing provides group communication through computers. It is the group version of electronic mail. Electronic mail systems are designed for person-to-person communication; filing of messages is by the individual. Computer-conferencing systems are geared toward groups; filing of messages is by group or by topic. Computer conferencing is a logical step toward computer-supported teams: once communication takes place through a computer, other forms of computer aids should be easier to add.

SCENARIO 10: INVISIBLE COLLEGE (SUPPORT FOR ELECTRONIC MEETINGS)

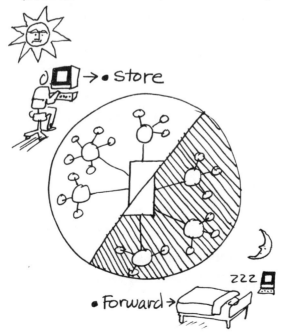

The team is close: they work together each day, and often some of them work into the night. The six team members are based in three countries and two states within one of the countries. The "time window" when they are all in their offices at once is very short. Thus, they usually work in a store-and-forward mode. They check the team's conference twice per day, see what has happened since they were there last, make their own comments, and leave. Drafts and other working documents, graphics, or models are also exchanged through the conferencing system.

CURRENT STATUS: Computer conferencing has been technically possible since about 1970, but few organizations have really taken advantage of its full potential. Commercial systems are currently available, but none is doing very well in the marketplace. Several private, in-house systems, however, are very successful. It has proved very difficult to get people used to computer conferencing as a general-purpose medium of communication.[8] The most likely path for the expansion of computer conferencing is through an expansion of existing electronic mail systems to include group-communication capabilities.

POSSIBLE PITFALLS: Computer conferencing appears to present more organizational than technical problems. In cases in which it has not worked out well, it typically has been introduced by a forward-thinking management information system (MIS) person who realizes quickly that such capabilities have more to do with a way of organizing work than they have with a computer system. Computer conferencing can easily create new channels of communication that might be quite different from formal organizational charts. MIS people typically have little training in organizational change, and that responsibility is certainly not part of their jobs. Thus, computer conferencing often is dropped after a trial, without ever achieving a "critical mass" of users within a company. Small teams can use computer conferencing without organizatonal support from their companies, but they must go through independent service providers to do so. (Indeed, small teams are the major clients of such services.) Most teams simply do not know such options exist, or they find them too expensive or too hard to organize.

11. Text-Filtering Software

Work teams often need large amounts of information that is hard to find. Text filtering allows users to search free-form or semistructured text, with more power achievable through more structure. Typically, users specify search criteria to be used by the filter. Text filtering can also be used to identify people with common interests. In this way, text filtering can be used for computer support of much larger communities, creating a kind of magnet for filtering text.

SCENARIO 11: NEEDLE IN A HAYSTACK (SUPPORT FOR ELECTRONIC MEETINGS)

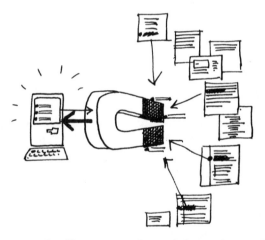

The team uses the filter to search out information and people that can help move its task forward. As is typical with many work teams, the members are working in a field that is still not mapped or well understood; they are ahead of the key words in traditional databases. The filter helps them specify just what kinds of information they want. Each morning, the filter prints a personalized "newspaper" for each team member, showing items from the preceding day's news, as well as new findings from the ongoing search for leads. Person-to-person messages also are filtered to insulate the team members from low-priority interruptions. The morning "paper" for the team leader contains a report on research just released in England, a priority message regarding continued funding, and a review of a new film he has been wanting to see.

CURRENT STATUS: Text filtering is being pursued most comprehensively by Tom Malone at MIT.[9] The original title of his experimental system was *electronic mail filter,* and it was intended to help users prioritize their incoming messages. Now his focus has broadened to an *information-lens* orientation, whereby the system reaches out to find information that matches the rules created by each user. Commercial systems for text filtering have not yet begun to appear, but there are definite indications of interest from both users and potential providers.

POSSIBLE PITFALLS: Text filtering is still more of a research vision than a commercial reality. Although the research is very encouraging, it is still research. The most promising short-run possibilities require much prestructuring of input from users; prestructuring means behavior changes in order to meet the requirements of the system. If teams pursue text filtering now instead of waiting for future improvements in capabilities, the requirements for prestructuring will be burdensome.

---

12. Computer-Supported Audio or Video Teleconferences

Another approach to computer-supported teams is to start with users who are already familiar with video teleconferencing. If they see merit in teleconferencing, it is likely that they will be open-minded about the potential for computer support for the electronic meetings they already hold.

SCENARIO 12: TELECONFERENCE ASSISTANT (SUPPORT FOR ELECTRONIC MEETINGS)

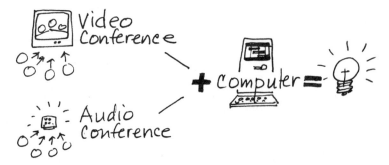

The regular Friday teleconference has just begun, and the budget glares back at the team members from the projection screen, with task overruns flashing in red. Each of the two video rooms has four team members present, all of whom are staring at the screens. "What do we do now? We've still got our deadline, but we don't have any money!"

The discussion centers on this question, with periodic recalculations and searches of parallel budgets to come up with additional funds. At the end of the meeting, the numbers are "frozen" for the team members to take along on paper copies. They have to keep working; next week they will decide whose budget gets hit for how much.

CURRENT STATUS: Computer use within teleconferences has been minimal to date. One computer manufacturer, however, uses projections of computer output during audio conferences in a fashion very similar to the scenario above. Also, several video teleconference rooms include personal computers on an experimental basis.

POSSIBLE PITFALLS: Video teleconferencing still is not a usual mode of business behavior. Adding computer support can serve to increase further the sense of technological discomfort felt by many users. For audio conferencing, the pitfalls can be similar to those noted in Scenario 9 for screen sharing.

---

13. Conversational Structuring

Communication among team members is a critical aspect of a team's performance, even though most groups do not consider how to structure this communication most effectively. One approach to computer-supported teams is to develop (or select) a structure for team conversations that will be in close keeping with the task and style of the team participants themselves. Structured conversations might provide both increased efficiency and effectiveness, if done well.

SCENARIO 13: SAY WHAT YOU MEAN (SUPPORT BETWEEN MEETINGS)

"OK, let's do it."
WHO SHOULD DO WHAT?
"I guess I should get it going."

WHAT WILL YOU DO, BY WHEN?
"I'll do it by Friday."
I'LL PUT IT ON YOUR CALENDAR
AND ADVISE THE REST OF THE TEAM.
WHAT, EXACTLY, ARE YOU AGREEING TO DO?

CURRENT STATUS: Conversational structuring is a quite different approach to software. It requires building explicit forms of communication about what most teams usually do in unstructured ways. The first commercial software to take a significant step toward conversational structuring is the Coordinator (by Action Technology of Emeryville, California).[10] We expect to see others within the next couple of years.

POSSIBLE PITFALLS: Structuring people's conversations is a risky business. It can be perceived as intrusive, or worse. Careful thought must be given to what structures make the most sense for a given work team, as well as how to introduce the structures once they have been selected. Also, some situations may actually benefit from ambiguity, or at least some team members may perceive this to be so.

14. Group Memory Management

Work teams have an obvious need for a group memory, particularly if individual members can search the memory in the ways they prefer (search methods are likely to vary among team members). The problems arise in structuring data to be retrieved as information by team members. Very flexible indexing structures are needed if this is to happen. The term *hypertext* has been used to describe nonlinear indexing structures that allow very flexible storage and retrieval options.

SCENARIO 14: PICKING UP THE FISHNET
(SUPPORT BETWEEN MEETINGS)

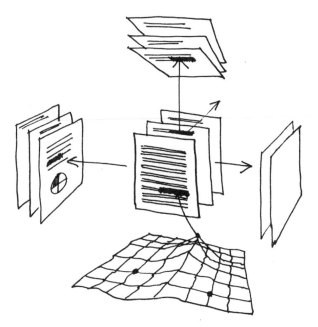

"I remember it was an idea we had a couple of months ago. I think it was Fred, and it had something to do with the notion of frequency." Sara fumes in frustration as she tries to remember the idea.

The Team Memory system contains notes from all the team meetings, with links among many of the words and concepts. Sara follows a weaving and bobbing path through words, data, and people in search of the lost idea. When she finally finds the idea, it is not nearly as good as she had remembered it. Her search process triggers a new idea for her, however, one that is much better than the original one.

CURRENT STATUS: Hypertext was coined by computer pioneer Ted Nelson in the mid-1960s, but it is only now making its way into regular (though certainly not yet common) use. Hypertext means that data can be stored and used in a computer in a way similar to how people now use a thesaurus. People do not read a thesaurus front to back, they follow links among words. Such an approach is much more flexible than typical hierarchical database structures common in today's computers. At this writing, Xerox's NoteCards system is one of the best working examples of hypertext, even though it is not being pushed as a commercial product. It is structured around the idea of working on index cards that can be linked and cross-referenced very easily.[11] Also, a hypertext system for the Macintosh, called Hypercards, is being distributed as systems software, meaning others can easily build on these capabilities. We expect many more hypertext systems to come on the market over the next several years. Hypertext systems have great potential for computer-supported teams. Ideally, hypertext capabilities will become an implicit part of software environments (like Hypercards in the Mac environment), rather than separate software. Hypertext should become "just something computers do," rather than a specialized function.

POSSIBLE PITFALLS: Hypertext is only now becoming understood and operationalized. Today's systems may be difficult for some teams to access, or difficult for them to use even if they can get to them. Also, this approach to indexing requires the creation of a new infrastructure for at least some aspects of team interaction: it will sometimes take major commitments at the front end to create the type of group memory that will prove useful down the line. Someone has to create all those hypertext links; it will take both discipline and skill.

15. Computer-Supported Spontaneous Interaction

It is often said that the most important team meetings happen around coffee pots, at water fountains, or in hallways. Can electronic systems be used to encourage and/or support such encounters?

SCENARIO 15: ELECTRONIC HALLWAY (SUPPORT BETWEEN MEETINGS)

It is almost midnight when Betsy is ready to log off the system. Just then, the system notifies her that Karen has logged on. They type messages to each other briefly before shifting to an audio link. (Neither of them is interested in a video link at midnight.) A long conversation ensues, the kind that rarely occurs at the office while everyone is rushing about.

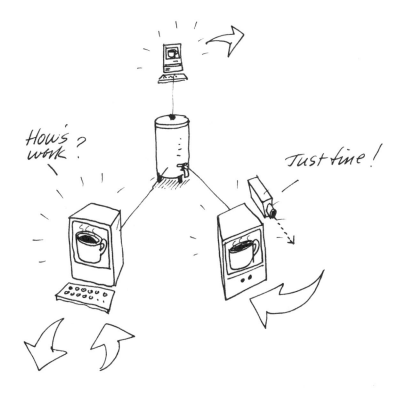

CURRENT STATUS: Canadian communications pioneer Gordon Thompson was one of the first to discuss the *electronic hallway* idea and its potential for influencing the formation and operation of groups.[12] The closest manifestation was the System Concepts Laboratory (SCL) at Xerox PARC. SCL was exploring computer-supported group technology and practice. Half the lab staff was physically located in Palo Alto, California, and half was in Portland, Oregon. Audio, video, and data links were available between the two groups 24 hours a day. The lab emphasized informal collaborative work for groups of two to ten people. The system allowed "drop-in" encounters over electronic media, much like what currently happens in hallways or around coffee pots.[13] Such communication is very important for work teams, and it certainly occurs much more frequently than do formal meetings in conference rooms.

POSSIBLE PITFALLS: The major hurdles here are logistical: how, specifically, do you go about creating an electronic hallway? Today's systems simply are not that portable or that flexible. Thus, the major pitfall can come from expecting too much too soon from this approach. In the long run, there is real promise, but this is a long-run approach.

---

16. Comprehensive Work Team Support

Work teams have many support needs, and toward the ambitious end of the spectrum, an integrated computer-based system is certainly attractive. Of course, comprehensive support is difficult to provide, even if the focus is on only one type of team. Still, this approach to groupware is an important direction that is becoming feasible. The general direction is toward putting users "inside" their computing environments.

Scenario 16: It's All Here (Support between Meetings)

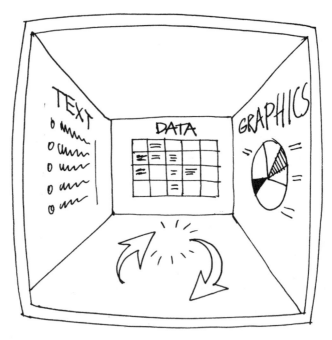

The competition is two weeks into a new advertising campaign that is particularly threatening to the brand team. The latest data are now in, and it is time to figure out what they mean. Each team member takes a crack at the analysis, sending along draft spreadsheet models and making statistical passes through the new data. Finally, they meet around a workstation, with one person doing the updates and final runs.

A summary briefing is then prepared for the brand manager, who receives the briefing and background data on her workstation 10 minutes before the meeting at which she is to decide how to respond to the competition.

CURRENT STATUS: The vision of comprehensive team support was first proposed by Douglas Engelbart in the early 1960s[14] Engelbart built a prototype system, NLS (for on*l*ine system), that still serves both as a benchmark and as a high-water mark. Movement from Engelbart's vision to commercial reality has been slow, however. (A commercial version of NLS has been available from McDonnell Douglas, but it has not been pushed.) The most significant step to date is focusing on brand teams in packaged goods industries, much like the scenario above. Metaphor Computer Systems (Mountain View, California) has an integrated system targeted specifically toward these types of high-performance teams. At this point, it seems reasonable to conclude that comprehensive team support can be provided best if it is geared toward specific types of teams, as with Metaphor.

POSSIBLE PITFALLS: With today's groupware products, users are likely to find that the specific functionality they achieve within an integrated system is not as powerful as that same functionality in a stand-alone system. This situation presents an unfortunate trade-off between the values of integration and power within specific functional areas. (This trade-off is not inevitable; it is certainly possible that integrated solutions can be more powerful than their stand-alone counterparts.) In addition to this trade-off, integrated systems are also likely to be expensive and probably are not compatible with the mainstream software marketplace.

17. Nonhuman Participants in Team Meetings

At some point, computer programs should be able to function, in some sense, as team "members." This approach to groupware grandiosity is the most ambitious in the list of 17 scenarios, and it relies heavily on developments in AI.

SCENARIO 17: NONHUMAN PARTICIPANTS (SUPPORT FOR ELECTRONIC MEETINGS)

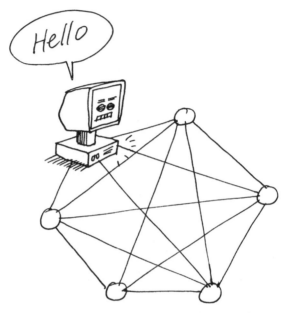

The team meeting for new brokers is just convening. Each trainee has spent the better part of the preceding day working with the Coach, an expert system that has specialized expertise about investment options the new brokers will be selling in another three weeks.

There are many opinions about investment options; even the Coach is only expressing an opinion. The new team discusses the options, consulting again with the Coach at several points during the meeting. The Coach has specialized knowledge that nobody on the team has, but it does not have definitive answers. It is a collaborative process, with all the team members (including the Coach) contributing.

CURRENT STATUS: No real-life examples of a computer program functioning as a team member are available, although there are several examples in user organizations (all proprietary) where similar ideas are being pursued. More detailed scenarios exist that introduce the concept of nonhuman participants and explore some of its implications.[15] There is also a growing interest among AI researchers in the role of expert systems as a knowledge medium, whereby people communicate through an expert system, rather than simply extracting information from it as an autonomous system.[16]

POSSIBLE PITFALLS: Designing systems that are thought of as "people" (or team "participants") may be quite misleading and perhaps counterproductive. Today's state of the art means that systems are a long way from personhood; this situation may always be so, or at least it is likely to be so for a long time to come. Care must be taken that the nonhuman participant is not oversold or misunderstood by human team members. In short, expectations must be managed within the realm of realism. This difficult scenario is very difficult to bring to life.

UNDERSTANDING WHAT IS GOING ON

What patterns can be seen across these 17 approaches to groupware? These approaches obviously cover a wide range of user activities. Although it is too early to conduct a detailed analysis of what is going on, it is useful to try out various categorizations of the current activities. First, Table 1 presents all 17 approaches in a single table,

Table 1   17 USER APPROACHES TO GROUPWARE
(FROM LEAST TO MOST DIFFICULT)

1. Face-to-face meeting facilitation services . . . Chauffeur
2. Group decision support systems . . . GDSS
3. Computer-based extensions of telephony for use by work groups . . . Telephone Extension
4. Presentation support software . . . Presentation Prep
5. Project management software . . . Team Conscience
6. Calendar management for groups . . . Our Black Book
7. Group-authoring software . . . Group Writing
8. Computer-supported face-to-face meetings . . . Beyond the White Board
9. PC screen-sharing software . . . Screen Sharing
10. Computer-conferencing systems . . . Invisible College
11. Text-filtering software . . . Needle in a Haystack
12. Computer-supported audio or video teleconferences . . . Teleconference Assistant
13. Conversational structuring . . . Say What You Mean
14. Group memory management . . . Picking up the Fishnet
15. Computer-supported spontaneous interaction . . . Electronic Hallway
16. Comprehensive work team support . . . It's All Here
17. Nonhuman participants in team meetings . . . Nonhuman Participants

arranged in approximate order of increasing difficulty. (The comparative difficulty of these approaches is, of course, debatable.)

Within the user approaches summarized in Table 1, it is possible to make a number of different groupings. Having tried many, we find it most useful to categorize the approaches according to one of the fundamentals of any work team, the meeting. We use a broad definition of "meeting" here, including any form of group interaction. The 17 approaches to groupware can be classified in the following fashion: support for face-to-face meetings, support for electronic meetings, and support between meetings. Table 2 presents this grouping.

Of course, some of the 17 scenarios could fall under more than one heading in Table 2. Scenario 13 (Conversational Structuring), for example, could fit under any of the three headings: support for face-to-face meetings, support for electronic meetings, or support

Table 2 CATEGORIZING THE 17 APPROACHES
BY MEETING SUPPORT

I. Support for Face-to-Face Meetings	
Scenario 1:	Facilitation services (Chauffeur)
Scenario 2:	Group decision support systems (GDSS)
Scenario 4:	Presentation support software (Presentation Prep)
Scenario 8:	Computer-supported meetings (Beyond the White Board)
II. Support for Electronic Meetings	
Scenario 3:	Extensions of telephony (Telephone Extension)
Scenario 9:	Screen-sharing software (Screen Sharing)
Scenario 10:	Computer conferencing (Invisible College)
Scenario 11:	Text filtering (Needle in a Haystack)
Scenario 12:	Audio or video teleconferencing (Teleconference Assistant)
Scenario 17:	Nonhuman participants (Nonhuman Participants)
III. Support between Meetings	
Scenario 5:	Project management software (Team Conscience)
Scenario 6:	Calendar management software (Our Black Book)
Scenario 7:	Group-authoring software (Group Writing)
Scenario 13:	Conversational structuring (Say What You Mean)
Scenario 14:	Group memory management (Picking up the Fishnet)
Scenario 15:	Spontaneous interaction (Electronic Hallway)
Scenario 16:	Comprehensive team support (It's All Here)

between meetings. I put it in the last category because I feel that is most important from a user point of view; that is, conversational structuring can help a team keep itself organized and on track with a structure that moves beyond specific team meetings.

Table 2 suggests that most of today's approaches to computer-supported groups are focused on electronic meeting support and support between meetings. These approaches also tend toward the middle and upper end of the difficulty spectrum (as indicated by the scenario numbers themselves, 1 through 17). Two of the options for face-to-face support are at the "easier" end of the spectrum (face-to-face facilitation and group decision support), as are one for electronic meeting support (building on the telephone) and three for support between meetings (calendar and project management, as well as group writing).

Classifying approaches to computer-supported teams according to support for team meetings is, of course, only one possibility. Table 3 regroups the 17 scenarios according to the group size they support. Although this book focuses on small business teams, 5 of the 17 scenarios provide their greatest advantages if they are employed within large organizations. For example, text filtering becomes increasingly valuable when there is more text to be filtered.

Table 3   CATEGORIZING THE 17 APPROACHES BY GROUP SIZE

Primary Advantage for Small Groups

Scenario 1:	Facilitation services (Chauffeur)
Scenario 2:	Group decision support systems (GDSS)
Scenario 3:	Extensions of telephony (Telephone Extension)
Scenario 5:	Project management software (Team Conscience)
Scenario 6:	Calendar management software (Our Black Book)
Scenario 7:	Group-authoring software (Group Writing)
Scenario 8:	Computer-supported meetings (Beyond the White Board)
Scenario 9:	Screen-sharing software (Screen Sharing)
Scenario 12:	Audio or video teleconferencing (Teleconference Assistant)
Scenario 14:	Group memory management (Picking up the Fishnet)
Scenario 16:	Comprehensive team support (It's All Here)
Scenario 17:	Nonhuman participants (Nonhuman Participants)

Primary Advantage for Large Groups

Scenario 4:	Presentation support software (Presentation Prep)
Scenario 10:	Computer conferencing (Invisible College)
Scenario 11:	Text filtering (Needle in a Haystack)
Scenario 13:	Conversational structuring (Say What You Mean)
Scenario 15:	Spontaneous interaction (Electronic Hallway)

Table 4 DISPLAY OF 17 SCENARIOS BY GEOGRAPHIC AND TIME DISPERSION OF PARTICIPANTS

	Time	
	Synchronous	*Asynchronous*
Face-to-face meetings	1. Facilitation services 2. Decision support 8. Beyond white board 17. Nonhuman participants	4. Presentation software 5. Project management 14. Memory management 16. Comprehensive support
Electronic meetings	3. Telephone extension 9. Screen sharing 12. Teleconference aid 15. Spontaneous interaction	6. Calendaring 7. Group writing 10. Computer conferencing 11. Text filtering 13. Conversation structuring

Another grouping of the 17 scenarios is displayed in Table 4, where a matrix is used to compare place and time of meetings. Synchronous meetings, in which all participants are present simultaneously, are not the only way groupware meetings can occur. Asynchronous communications allow team members to communicate according to their own schedules in a store-and-forward mode. We feel that asynchronous communications capabilities will be one of the most compelling features of many groupware products. Even though asynchronous meetings are still foreign to most business users, 8 of the 17 scenarios emphasize this form of team communications.[17] (It should be noted that the classification of scenarios by face-to-face or electronic meetings is based upon my judgment regarding where the primary benefit lies; some scenarios can be employed with either face-to-face or electronic meetings.)

The preceding 17 approaches to groupware represent a wide span of current user views. As stated earlier, there are definite overlaps among the approaches, but each represents a valid starting point of frame of reference for users as they consider computer support for business teams. We expect that clear successes will occur for several of the approaches (probably more than half), that combinations of approaches will prove even more successful in the long run, and that new approaches will emerge as it becomes more possible for users to experiment with groupware options.

CHAPTER 3

Current Vendor Approaches to Groupware

ROBERT JOHANSEN AND ROBERT MITTMAN

No large-scale groupware market exists today, but some early products and product classes could serve as attractive points of departure for market growth. There are also existing market segments that could serve as a technological base for groupware or that have groupware "hooks" already built in.

In this chapter, we discuss several product categories that are at the core of vendors' approaches to groupware. All of them are available (though often in limited ways) in today's marketplace; most of them emphasize features other than groupware. We offer this classification as a "straw man" to consider, argue with, and perhaps improve upon. Some of these categories have more to do with groupware than others, though at this stage, it is too early to know which.

Five current product classes appear to be the most probable building blocks for groupware:

Products for synchronous collaborative communication

Extensions of existing software products

Messaging, voice mail, conferencing, and other store-and-forward products and services

Local area networks (LANs)

Departmental computing.

Additionally, several categories that are less central to groupware may nevertheless have an impact on its development:

Note: This chapter benefited greatly from work and discussions with Elliot Gold, JoAnne Goldberg, and Dick Roistacher.

Public network services

PBXs

Add-on and peripheral devices for personal computers

Integrated voice/data workstations.

The diversity of technologies in the foregoing list should make it clear that the current state of the groupware market is diffuse and uncertain. Unlike many technologies that are well defined, it is not yet clear what is groupware and what is not. Groupware seems likely to emerge, but from where?

To prospective users, groupware provides ideas about how communication might take place, but there are few available products—at least not yet. To vendors, groupware is a perception of what users want, combined with new capabilities their technologies can offer. Many of the technological developments are taking place far from where people now use systems. Those who want to push technology to meet more advanced needs must delve deeper into the technological details than most of them care to go.

This environment is bound to change. Groupware concepts will find their way into the mainstream. Users will have to look less hard to find groupware products; vendors will understand groupware needs better. Eventually, groupware features will become part of other products.

One very promising vehicle for new electronic group communications is the PC, one of the most successful products of the century. The other logical building block for groupware is even more ubiquitous: the telephone. It seems apparent that virtually every office worker will, within the next 10 years, have access to computing power (a workstation or a PC) from his or her desk. Office workers will be using these devices for writing, for planning, for developing graphic materials, for making decisions—and for communicating. Why not group communication?

Of course, no one—the vendors or the users—has a similar single concept of what the PC is. With all the software being developed for it today, it can look like a typewriter to a secretary, an electronic spreadsheet to an accountant, a CAD system to an engineer, or a management tool to a project manager. We see this lack of agreement as a hurdle for groupware, but it also suggests an openness regarding what the PC might become. Certainly the telephone, in the definitional stage 100 years ago, was seen differently by its early users. Even today, it is seen, for example, as an order entry device by merchants, a social tool by teenagers, and a screening device by executives with secretaries.

The *concept* of using personal computers for communications is not new. Many of them are sold with modems and communications software. Others are linked in local or wide-area networks. A few products are designed for augmenting interpersonal communication among computer users.

Technology is an important dynamic of the groupware market. Advanced communications and computer technology, coupled with the continuing development of standards, is fundamental to the future of groupware. Technology can enhance the user/product interface, which is critical for product acceptance.

Vendors play a key role in the groupware market. They include computer manufacturers, software vendors, communications companies, and various peripheral manufacturers. Most of the vendors are small companies that have not been in the marketplace previously and are seeking a niche. Although many of these newer vendors have innovative ideas, most of them do not have the capital or managerial expertise to achieve a high degree of business success. In this book, we mention only a few providers and products that are relatively stable. The names and the players are changing quickly, and our goal is to look beyond the transiencies of the current marketplace to the future of groupware.

Some groupware products have found small numbers of enthusiastic users. Such early adopters constitute a small percentage of the potential market, but they have two important roles. Their work serves as early market research (formal or informal) for refining products that would be unacceptable to a less-forgiving general market. They also prepare the public mind to accept the more-mature versions of products. A few users are actively engaged in designing their own products, developing tools for themselves that others may use later. As the market continues to grow, the types of users and the types of applications for which they use communication products will also increase.

In some of these product areas, the best efforts of users, vendors, and technologists will not be enough to create successful products. External competition—that is, competition among different classes of products—may overwhelm a product before it gains acceptance. Further, exogenous forces may change the conditions the product was designed to address. These forces include changes in society and in organizational structure that can affect the development of the market. Such forces also tend to interact with the market forces: computers create change in the structure of an organization; the change in the structure requires an adjustment in the computer system. Exogenous forces are difficult to assess, and projections are, at best, highly speculative. Nevertheless, it is useful for anyone looking at the groupware market to track external forces that may have significant impacts on market development.

These ideas—concept, technology, vendors, users, and competitive issues—provide a framework for understanding the product classes identified above. Table 5 summarizes how each current product class stacks up. The rest of this chapter examines each area in more depth.

COLLABORATIVE/SHARED WORKSPACES

Collaborative and shared workspaces is the current product class that most closely resembles our concept of groupware. Products in this class enable two or more people in remote locations or in a single location to work together more effectively through specialized electronic media. Two types of collaborative systems are entering the market—software products that allow the sharing of text, data, graphics, and other information in multiple locations and electronic aids to support communication in face-to-face meetings.

Shared-screen software packages require communications adapters and modems on the PCs on which they run. Several of them require special hardware, such as a mouse or graphics tablet (see Chapter 2, Scenario 9 for an example). The complexities of the systems, however, are software related. If more than one user can access a given workspace, sophisticated networking protocols are necessary. Even if network protocols are not developed, products can have ways of enforcing rules for participation, passing leadership ("passing the chalk"), and ordering agendas and lists of ideas.

Room-based collaborative systems provide a set of electronic tools to enhance face-to-face communication. These include graphics aids, group memory tools, brainstorming aids, and links to external data

Table 5 THE CURRENT GROUPWARE PRODUCT CLASSES

Product Categories	Concept	Technology	Vendors	Users	Competitive Issues
Collaborative/ shared workspaces	Work-group computing	Specialized software and hardware	Entrepreneurs; a few large companies	Specialized need	Selling the concept
Software extensions	Groupware as a new feature	Software add-ons	Software vendors	Software users	Search for next winner
Electronic messaging	Store-and-forward messaging	Text and voice messaging	Entrepreneurs; a few large companies	Varied	Behavior changes
LANs	Local computer communications	PCs; networks	Small and large hardware companies	Varied	Standards compatibility
Departmental computing	Shared computing resources	Minicomputers or PCs	Hardware companies	Departments; projects	Mainframes; networks
Network services	Public services	Networks	Carriers; networks	Varied	Overcapacity; regulation
PBXs	Local voice and data switching	Telephony	Large companies	Large and medium companies	LANs for data; price and features
Add-ons and peripherals	PC extensions	Images; graphics; communications	Hardware companies; entrepreneurs	Specialized need	Other media
Integrated workstations	All in one box	Integrated hardware	Hardware companies; entrepreneurs	Specialized need	Components versus package; price

49

sources. Electronic blackboards (or white boards) can form the core of such systems. But they also may include individual keyboard inputs, large-screen computer monitors, videoconferencing links to other locations, and other aids. Although they are designed primarily for real-time communications, these systems may also have store-and-forward capabilities.

There are many problems inherent in a collaborative system. The primary problem is that current collaborative systems often require users to have a significant amount of computer sophistication. Their successful use also requires the participants to have a fairly close and positive working relationship with each other. These systems do, indeed, seem to be collaborative, in that they are most effective with users who can think and work together well.

The most serious competitive technologies can be split into two groups. For those products that permit users to be in different locations, strong competition comes from most of the other product areas described in this book, most of which (at this stage) are easier to understand and easier to use than are collaborative systems. For those products that require users to be in close proximity, the strongest competition comes from the blackboard, white board, or flip-chart pad. Users are being asked to buy not merely a particular product but a new way of working through computers. (See Scenarios 1 and 8, Chapter 2 for examples.)

These products have not been, for the most part, driven by the external market. Instead, their development has resulted from a perceived need by developers for such a tool. Because many of these products are not available generally, current users are often members of a small, self-selected group; often, the users are the developers.

The developers and vendors of these types of products tend to be small, entrepreneurial organizations—or entrepreneurial subgroups within larger organizations. The most elaborate collaborative systems are produced by research groups, both as research projects and as tools for facilitating the group's work. Most of these products are not yet commercially available. In the longer run, we expect large software houses, telecommunications providers, and computer manufacturers to become involved. Some of the more-established vendors are forming cooperative arrangements with start-up companies.

Collaborative software can be valuable for people working closely together to answer a complex question or to contribute to a project.

Trends toward decentralized organizations and global markets will make such tools more practical in the future.

SOFTWARE EXTENSIONS

Because presenting groupware as stand-alone collaborative systems is difficult, it may be easier to sell groupware capabilities as a feature added to a product that users already understand. For example, if group writing (Scenario 7 in Chapter 2) were offered as a simple extension of word-processing software, it would provide an easier purchase decision for prospective customers. In fact, group-writing features are now starting to appear in popular word-processing programs. A similar argument could be made for group-oriented spreadsheet programs that remember who made which changes in what cells. The concept here is selling at the margins of a successful product, selling a new feature rather than a completely new product. Groupware functions could be added quite easily to a number of existing classes of software products.

In the typical cycle of software development of an existing product, users of a product react to the current version. They point out software bugs, identify shortcomings, and ask for new features. At the same time, developers look at competing products and other software to find features to incorporate in the next release. Groupware features must compete with others for developers' attention. In many cases, groupware features are not a simple development—they introduce the complexity of giving several users access to the same workspace or document.

Who uses a groupware product depends on the specific application being extended. In fact, the extension might imply some changes in end users of the product. For example, a group-writing product built upon a word-processing package may mean that managers start using the program, along with their secretaries. This could imply a larger market, but it might also imply some redesign to the product to make it attractive to the additional users.

The competitive environment for software is frenzied. There is a constant search for the next big winner. Games, spreadsheets, and word processors have been hits in the past. The next big winner might be a group-oriented product. Thus, there will be strong competitive pressures and great interest in whatever early efforts are attempted.

ELECTRONIC MESSAGING PRODUCTS AND SERVICES

Electronic messaging, including both electronic mail and computer conferencing, is another class of products that could have great potential. The basic concept here is typed text messages exchanged among group members, with each participant checking for messages periodically. Some systems provide automatic delivery if messages are not picked up. They represent the most obvious adaptations of the office keyboard to communications: anyone with a communicating keyboard can link into a system to exchange messages. Viewed as an alternative to paper messaging, electronic messaging has a major advantage: it is fast. Prices established by commercial vendors have also been reasonable; they cannot really compete with the cost of a first-class letter, but their cost are much lower than those charged for express delivery services.

In addition to these commercial services, many organizations have developed in-house systems. The primary disadvantage of this type of system is apparent: it can only be used by people who can access the internal network. For this reason, gateways to the outside world are becoming more common and more flexible. A consolidated directory listing participants in many electronic mail services has been introduced. This kind of "white pages" for electronic mail users makes it easier for uses on different systems to communicate.

Computer conference systems differ from electronic mail systems in two major ways. First, the messages in the system are kept in a central, shared repository, rather than in individual mailboxes. Second, the system has facilities for indexing, sequencing, and cross-referencing the messages to form a more integrated set of proceedings.

The use of computer messaging and conferencing is highly skewed, with pockets of extensive use and large numbers of registered users who make little or no use of the system. If an organization has a critical mass of users, obtaining new users becomes easier; however, very few organizations have been able to generate adequate managerial and office staff support to create that critical mass.

There has been quite a bit of effort to promote message standards, the most promising of which is called CCITT X.400 (CCITT is an international standards organization); it includes formats for exchange across systems. X.400 has been endorsed by a number of organizations and is becoming an international standard. The result will be greatly increased capabilities for exchanging electronic messages across systems.

Voice mail is a different manifestation of the same electronic messaging perspective. Voice mail is simply a more sophisticated form of the telephone answering machine, one in which the message can be stored, sorted, and returned with computer support. It is based on equipment available to virtually all office users—the telephone. The market is still small, but some observers claim that it is growing much more rapidly than most other segments of telecommunications. Most voice mail systems are integrated with existing telephone systems on the customer's premises. As its name suggests, voice mail permits users to call anyone on the system and leave a voice message. With some systems, the message recipient is notified by a message-waiting indicator on the telephone and can then play back the message.

The limiting problem with voice messaging has been one of digitizing and storing the voice. Early systems had very poor message quality and required large computer storage. The decreasing costs of disk storage and the advances in the digital encoding of voice have solved many qualitative problems in voice messaging. Costs of storage will continue to decrease; people will continue to develop more efficient digitizing techniques.

The high start-up costs have discouraged some potential users from purchasing voice mail. Despite its relative simplicity, there is (as with all innovation) a certain degree of user resistance. Nevertheless, voice mail is becoming popular among employees of organizations that have adopted it. There is frustration regarding links to other computer-based messaging systems, however.

Both voice mail and computer messaging and conferencing are sold as products and services. They can be bought as software packages and installed on customers' computers or used on a fee-for-service basis. An electronic message service is offered by most of the data common carrier companies. Voice mail, as noted, is most frequently sold in conjunction with an existing communication system. Voice mail vendors also sell stand-alone systems that can be added to existing telephone systems or used independently. In addition, simple voice mail systems are becoming available as expansion boards for PCs.

Some interesting hybrids of electronic mail and voice mail will develop in the future. Electronic mailboxes can easily be hooked to a voice synthesizer. The user will simply dial in from a telephone and listen to synthesized readings from the mailbox. (Note that the opposite service—turning a voice message into text—will take far longer to develop; the practical voicewriter is not around the corner.) Standards like X.400 can be extended to voice mail and even messages in other media. A multimedia workstation can play messages back in whatever medium they were sent.

The greatest competitive threat to electronic messaging comes from the plain old telephone. White-collar workers often spend a large portion of their day on the telephone; the telephone is reliable, serves its purpose, and engenders little incentive to shift to a more complicated, high-technology method of communications. (Telephone tag, the problem of leaving messages rather than having a conversation, is probably the major telephone pain that encourages users to explore messaging systems.)

The primary external force is the perceived universality of electronic communication systems. The customer needs to be convinced that everyone he or she wants to talk to, as well as all competitors, is already hooked up to the system. Electronic mail directories are a major step toward reaching this critical mass.

Another force is the corporate culture of a given organization. Members of senior management may be reluctant to use such a system because it represents an increased adoption of technology (many senior managers are leery of untried technologies). It also requires a dramatic increase in intraorganizational communication and a concomitant rise in the number of people involved in decision processes. An organization must be flexible enough to accept the possibility that a communications system might alter the nature of everyday operations. Many organizations are not that flexible.

LOCAL AREA NETWORKS

LANs permit users to hook PCs in a single location (and usually in a single organization) together in a network. The most frequent motivation for LANs is to give many users shared access to costly peripherals such as laser printers, high-speed modems, and mass storage. A second use of LANs is to improve users' access to software. A wide range of software products can be offered on the network. Further, a network manager can be certain that all users have updated software without having to collect and distribute diskettes. (For this reason, LANs can offer increased security over uncontrollable floppy disks.) Finally, a LAN can give users easy access to the same files. This function, combined with electronic mail or screen-sharing software on the LAN, can form the core of LAN-based groupware.

The standards for local area networking, long an area of some dispute, have been settled, or so it would seem. The two standards represent a shotgun marriage between two completely different philosophies of network management. In the usual division of such things, almost everyone but IBM has gone to a standard called *Ethernet,* while IBM has introduced what it calls a *token ring network.* A promising development is the availability of simple and inexpensive LAN equipment that links IBM PCs to Apple Macintoshes. They make available some of the desktop publishing capabilities of the Apple to the large installed base of IBM users.

LANs are primarily applied in a single geographic location. Some users, however, are experimenting with linking LANs. This development holds promise for groupware applications in multiple locations.

LAN sales have increased rapidly, with nearly half a million in use in 1987. Moreover, the average number of PCs connected to a LAN will increase as additional PCs are added to existing LANs and as newly purchased LANs grow larger. Several factors limit the diffusion of LANs. Chief among them is wiring cost. Although the LAN server and cabling may be purchased at a relatively low cost, installation costs may be prohibitive, especially in older buildings.

Another barrier for LAN diffusion is the difficulty of network management. Poor PC hygiene—out-of-date software, messy disk directories, insufficient backups—remains a hidden problem in non-networked computers. A LAN is like a crowded subway car—one person's poor hygiene is felt by everyone. A network manager must be appointed to keep the system operating smoothly. Even with a network manager, groupware use of LANs may cause unforeseen problems. In particular, when many people work on a single document, it is crucial to identify who makes what changes, what is the most current version of the document, and who controls the document. Software can help, but changes in procedures and work style are surely needed.

DEPARTMENTAL COMPUTING

Departmental computing grew out of end-user computing. It came from a realization that too much *personal* computing just did not make sense in many situations. Departmental computing is a sharing of computing resources among a group of users, even if they are not a formal department. In scale, departmental computing lies between time-shared computing (in which large mainframe computers are shared among many users) and networked PCs. The key concept for departmental computing is the notion of sharing computer resources while still allowing as much computing power to reside with the user as makes sense in a given situation.

In most of today's departmental computing environments, users are treated more as aggregations of individuals than as groups; that is, applications are geared toward individual users—even though the computer resources are actually being shared across users. The users of departmental computing systems are not necessarily collaborating, as is implied by the groupware concept. There is real potential, however, for departmental computing systems to deliver groupware services over the infrastructure they have developed.

The technology for departmental computing systems can come from either of two directions: expanded PCs or minicomputers functioning as central hosts. With the expanded power of PCs, the former option is becoming easier and more popular.

Computer vendors such as IBM, Digital Equipment Corporation, and Hewlett-Packard have product lines focused on departmental computing. Various PCs can also be configured to work well in a departmental computing environment. In some sense, users have a choice of PC plus or mainframe minus. These are two different angles on the departmental computing marketplace, but the end result is often quite similar in terms of capabilities—no matter which angle is being employed. The vendors do tend to vary, depending on which angle is taken, however.

The obvious users of departmental computing are departments. The definition of department within a user organization can vary widely, however. Some departments might involve hundreds of users; others may be more the size of project teams. The important characteristic is that all the users share some common needs for computing resources and some common access to the actual machine(s) being used.

The competitive environment for departmental computing is quite intense. Personal computing caught most manufacturers off guard, and departmental computing represents something of a return to stability, or at least familiarity. Large computer manufacturers are used to making machines that many people use. Departmental computing is much closer to the making machines that many people use. Departmental computing is much closer to the mainframe model than is the renegade PC world. In one way, this is good news for manufacturers, but many competitors also would like to benefit from the good news. There is, of course, competition from network service providers and mainframe providers, each of whom might offer similar services to some users. Also, the dramatic increases in PC power has meant that users can "build their own" departmental computer system much more easily than used to be the case.

The announcement in early 1988 that Digital and Apple will jointly develop products that integrate VAXes and Macintoshes is a bellwether. The lines between PCs and departmental computing will continue to blur as more functions, such as file sharing, electronic mail, and document interchange, are done transparently between the two environments.

As for external trends affecting departmental computing, decentralization is again very important. User organizations have strong needs for departmental support, often across large distances. Even in local areas, decentralized organizational forms are becoming more popular than central corporate resources. Such divisionalization creates a very favorable climate for departmental computing.

From a groupware point of view, departmental computing is very attractive indeed. In effect, departmental computing provides a set of "highways" that can be used directly by groupware applications. In such an environment, groupware providers can focus on the specific capabilities they are offering, rather than on the means through which those capabilities are delivered (which is often a showstopper in cases where the "highways" are not already in place).

NETWORK SERVICES

Network-based services encompass a broad range of areas, most of which are transparent to the user. If groupware services can be imbedded in a network, users can pay for each use, rather than making a large initial investment. A variety of network developments are making the appearance of such services more likely. Telephone companies are obvious candidates for offering such services, but so are computer network companies. For example, screen sharing could be offered as an addition to telephone conference calls, or group writing could be provided as a network service.

Gateway services are an important product concept that network providers are considering, and some are already offering them. A great potential exists here for networks to join together disparate systems in a fashion that looks fully integrated to the user. Judge Greene's September 1987 revision of the modified final judgment for the Bell System divestiture allowed the regional Bell operating companies (often called RBOCs) to offer gateway services. Much development interest will center on this area in the next few years.

Although current interest is focused on networks, it seems apparent that long-term concerns will be related to value-added services. Vendors who can take raw bandwidth and shape it into a viable product (as in the gateway services) may find a receptive market. The configuration of such products and services is yet to be determined.

A key development in the mid-1990s will be the diffusion of the integrated services digital network (ISDN). ISDN promises to put two data and voice channels over the conventional twisted-pair wire that connects every telephone. The implications for groupware are substantial, because a single telephone line can transmit text, graphics, data, and voice simultaneously. Even before ISDN reaches wide diffusion, data over voice (DOV) technologies will give users the chance to transmit text and graphics at the same time a voice conversation is in progress.

A discussion of the technology of network-based services is beyond the scope of this book. Advances in such technology, however, have two effects. They provide the use of expensive facilities to users who could not otherwise afford them, thus expanding the scope of the users' communication networks. As the technology advances, less-expensive devices become available for sale to users. Media saturation also will serve to reduce prices.

Providers of network services tend to be major communications companies. Smaller, newer companies have entered the market in specialized areas: several of the satellite network operators are relatively small organizations.

Although all end users of communications services ultimately benefit from implementation of advanced network technology, the immediate purchasers of network services tend to be large companies—for example, Citibank, ARCO, J.C. Penney, and Merrill Lynch.

The major force in this market is related to the fact that there may well be overcapacity in the marketplace by the early 1990s. Only 60 percent of available fiber optic capacity is currently in use, yet new cable is being laid. By 1990, about 100,000 miles of optical fiber will be laid in the ground if all current plans are executed. This is more than 10 times the amount used today.

PRIVATE BRANCH EXCHANGES

PBX systems are used by medium and large organizations to provide enhanced telephone service to their employees. The user base for this equipment is virtually universal: almost every organization with more than 30 or 40 people has a PBX or is tied to Centrex (a telephone network alternative to the PBX). As the vendors incorporate increasingly more-sophisticated features into their equipment, users who purchase new equipment will benefit from the most-advanced technological enhancements. When the users realize the power available through their PBX systems, they may choose to exploit it. By using such a system as a foundation for computer-based communications, groupware is a new feature that can be added at a relatively low marginal cost.

The PBX market is dominated by major companies: AT&T, Northern Telecom, Rolm, and Mitel. This is a multibillion dollar market, with no room for underfinanced competition. New and small companies can penetrate the market through offering enhancements (such as voice mail systems) to the PBX vendors for incorporation into the end product.

Competition among individual vendors is fierce, with features and price being the main selling points. We expect to see increased emphasis on integration of communications components, the development of advanced office applications, and compatibility with computer equipment.

Competition in the communications common carrier market combined with new technologies such as fiber optics might make new types of connections feasible. For example, companies with close working relationships might find it profitable to integrate their internal communication systems via a high-bandwidth common carrier.

Such an integration might affect company decisions on internal communication networks, such as those supported by PBXs and LANs.

ADD-ON AND PERIPHERAL DEVICES

This category includes graphics boards that can be installed in a PC, cameras, voice digitizers, and other hardware add-ons. Most products in this category have specialized purposes. To be used as groupware, they may require modems, additional software, or larger displays. Still, they may enhance the use of PCs for groupware, because multimedia capabilities are often very useful to groups.

The high-resolution graphics board is perhaps the best established of the products. These boards, which can be easily plugged into a PC, allow the screen to be painted with lines and shapes, as well as printed with characters. Such boards make it possible to use the computer as a graphic display device. Some collaboration systems depend on shared graphics and on the ability for people to use the screen as a blackboard. More sophisticated add-ons include products that make the computer roughly equivalent to a primitive sort of freeze-frame device. By adding a camera and other peripherals to the computer, the user can transmit images to other users. Voice digitizers, though not necessarily independent of the other products in this category or in the first category, add an extra channel to the conferencing activity by permitting voice transmission over a data line.

AT&T (Indianapolis), OPTEL (New York City), and others have developed expansion boards and expansion console devices that make PCs the engines behind groupware systems. At this time, these systems bring messaging, audiographics, and captured frame video functions to the PC. As the 32-bit processor begins to be incorporated into hardware, we can expect to see things that border on motion video and image database systems for PC conferencing. Apple's Macintosh and IBM's PS/2 line, for example, have enhanced graphics and image-processing capabilities which we expect will be used as a platform for groupware.

To protect their lead in the business markets, IBM, Compaq, and Apple with its Macintosh II have gone to an open architecture. These manufacturers have published the information that allows other companies to design expansion boards for their machines. In doing so, they hope to amplify their dominance by showing that their product is the best buy in terms of price and function. If they have a significant installed base, they can attract the expansion-board manufacturers who will increase their performance. With the increased performance, the PC manufacturers can make more sales.

Users of these products currently fall into the early innovator or experimenter group. Some PC enthusiasts purchase such products to add capabilities (which they may not use extensively) to their machines.

The greatest competition comes from other forms of PC linkages. There are problems with each end of the peripheral spectrum. At the low end, the add-on boards have limited capabilities, yet they require a certain amount of hardware sophistication. At the high end, the products have more flexibility (PCs as engines for freeze-frame systems, for example), but they are commensurately more expensive. The difficulty of dealing with the hardware may dissuade potential users. Moreover, increasingly sophisticated PBX/LAN equipment may make much of this equipment obsolete.

This equipment is designed to supplement the underlying hardware, the PCs themselves. The vendors of these add-ons generally have little control over the development of the machines themselves. Therefore, as computers continue to evolve fairly rapidly, it may be increasingly difficult for the add-on vendors to keep their products compatible with the equipment.

INTEGRATED WORKSTATIONS

Integrated voice and data workstations have been the topic of a considerable amount of speculation. Initially, the concept was regarded as a brilliant maneuver: the combination of all electronic desktop devices into one integrated package. No more separate boxes for the telephone, computer, modem, loudspeaker, Rolodex, answering machine, message slips, and assorted other miscellany. With a workstation it would be possible to make telephone calls, look up information, and send messages with just a few keystrokes: an ideal tool for the busy manager. Integrated workstations, however, have been tough to build and tough to sell.

Integrated voice and data workstations may be money savers, costing less than the combined price of a PC and a "smart" telephone; in most cases, however, they cost considerably more than minimum cost alternatives. They may save desk space, not a trivial consideration, given the cost and scarcity of office space in many areas. With proper linkages, users may increase productivity by obtaining information quickly and efficiently. On the subjective side of the ledger, a workstation can enhance job satisfaction and ultimately increase the competitive edge of a corporation.

In the simplest case, the workstation does little more than serve as a telephone dialer. In more elaborate systems, the workstation does many things in both the computing and telephony worlds. Some manufacturers of integrated workstations have been adding various voice capabilities, most of which involve the digitizing and storage of voice. Another voice feature being added to some workstations is voice synthesis. Thus, the workstation can offer verbal prompts when the display is entirely occupied by some other feature. Speech recognition and understanding are far more difficult to do than voice storage and synthesis. We doubt that integrated workstations will have any more than rudimentary speech recognition capabilities in the foreseeable future.

The workstation product market is a curious one. Most of the major companies in communications/computing, such as AT&T and IBM, have been slow to enter the area. Although some market leaders are active in this area (notably Northern Telecom), the acceptance of integrated workstations is still far below expectations. The newer companies are struggling as a result of low sales volume, poor distribution networks, and unsatisfactory pricing policies. Small, innovative companies seem to have three paths: they can seek to become large companies with stable user bases (a longshot nowadays); they can be acquired by or enter into long-term supply relations with large companies; or they can look for a specialized niche. Some of the more prominent of the venture-capital-funded enterprises have been forced to file for bankruptcy protection under Chapter 11. Other start-ups, such as Sun Microsystems (Mountain View, California) and Metaphor Computer Systems (Mountain View, California) have developed a positive business image and are favorably regarded; they have strong niches—Sun for scientific users and Metaphor for brand teams in the packaged-goods industry.

The most serious competitive problem is the problem of packaging: whether or not to market a closed system to which the user cannot add any hardware or software not provided by the vendor. Such a situation is unattractive to most customers, especially those who have already invested in PCs. But vendors are caught in a dilemma. If a vendor attempts a totally closed system, then few customers will make the commitment to adopting the system. If the vendor allows an open architecture, then the user can build cheaper (and perhaps better) workstations by adding some hardware and software to standard PCs.

External forces influencing the evolution of workstations focus on changes in corporate culture. For example, the target group for most workstation vendors (managers and professionals) is gradually becoming more accepting of computers and may be more willing to deal with the intricacies of a workstation. Part of the value of workstations is their ability to do things jointly with other workstations. It makes sense to sell workstations to people who can use them to interact with other workstation users. Sales may spread from division to division in large companies. As standards are established, it may be possible to link compatible workstations in different companies. This is an ambitious vision, however, and it is difficult to be optimistic about how quickly it will occur. Groupware will play a role in the vision, but it is likely to be a long time in coming—except for specific segments of the market.

SUMMARY

There is no single dominant groupware concept, although a few likely possibilities are starting to emerge. Concepts span a broad range of price and functionality. The dominant concepts will be a function of the interplay among technological, vendor, user, competitive, and exogenous forces.

Unsurprisingly, the technologies that characterize this market come from two major sources: the communications industry and the computer industry. The most troublesome aspect of the market is that no set of technologies exists that have been pulled together to create an overwhelmingly successful product. The PC had such a success when the Apple II (a PC) met VisiCalc (an application of PCs to spreadsheets). It did things that nothing else in that price range did, and the consumer had to buy only one of each to do them. Groupware needs a similar convergence of technology and application.

Several technological developments merit watching because of their potential impact on groupware:

Computer-Related Developments

The availability of larger and cheaper processors and main memories will enhance the capabilities—and speed—of computer-based operations.

Improved storage facilities, such as optical disks and the increasingly common hard disks with large capacity will increase the amount and type of information that can be stored and retrieved. It is conceivable that video disk storage will provide enough cheap capacity to allow continuous monitoring and recording of communications activity.

Increasing competition in the software market will motivate vendors to produce software that operates more efficiently and that has more features.

AI/expert systems will be increasingly important. There is a growing emphasis on the development of AI tools that enable users to tailor applications to their specific needs. AI may provide adaptive user interfaces, thereby making the computer more accessible. (Chapter 5 explores this connection in more detail.)

Voice synthesis will enable more "natural" interfaces to the computer.

Communications-Related Developments

Faster, cheaper modems (for sending computer signals over telephone lines) will make it possible to transmit large quantities of information quickly.

Large-scale adoption of LANs will permit greater intraorganization electronic communication and the sharing of computer resources.

ISDNs promise to provide easy telephone network gateways and channels between local networks, erasing the perceived distinction between local and remote computer communications. Pre-ISDN alternatives such as data over voice permit users to transmit data on phone lines without disrupting voice communications.

Bypass networks offer alternative, possibly cheaper, and sometimes more flexible methods of communication—cellular, fiber optics, and satellite, for example.

In the product areas that focus directly on the facilitation of electronic communication through use of a computer, vendors are largely new or recently established companies. Most offer software packages and hardware devices designed to operate on office PCs. The major communications and computer companies are just beginning to explore the groupware territory.

It is important to consider the potential impact of the major communications and computer vendors. They are certain to exert a profound influence over the developing market, because they control most of the communications networks, establish the protocols, and have access to immense distribution systems.

It is likely that many of the better, smaller companies will be acquired by major communications and computer companies seeking to fill a market niche. This would provide the smaller companies with the capital and management expertise necessary to establish their innovative products in the marketplace.

The users of each of the classes of product have tended to be early adopters of technology in general and PCs in particular. The increasing popularity of graphically oriented computers such as the Apple Macintosh and the IBM PS/2 is a promising development for the spread of groupware: complex group activities can be well represented in a graphics environment. If computers become widely used for interpersonal communication, a larger market will open. Alternatively, one of the established office systems may serve as a core for computer/communications functionalities.

The most significant force affecting the overall market is user acceptance. The question of acceptance is tricky. The PC—as an office tool—may be a ubiquitous beast, but its presence still causes discomfort among many. If groupware is to be accepted, it must either become transparent to the user (that is, that its complex operations are automatic and built into the system, so that the user need not know they are taking place), or the user must be so familiar with electronic equipment that its mastery is no longer mildly terrifying and its use is more rewarding than frustrating. It is likely that acceptance will occur when the equipment becomes easier to use and when there is something approaching universality of access. Fundamental user habits and attitudes are much less flexible, and vendors should not expect potential clients to greet innovation enthusiastically.

The most important exogenous force is the changing nature of management structures. Organizations are changing, partly as a result of technological influences, partly because of social and cultural forces. Some observers argue that organizations are becoming flatter and leaner; others see operations becoming increasingly complex and convoluted. The nature of structural changes, particularly those affecting management, will have a substantial impact on the acceptance of groupware.

This chapter emphasized the current product classes, not specific products or users. The technology is available; the market potential exists. Current product classes can grow into groupware—or vice versa—if the connection between user needs and vendor offerings can be made convincingly.

CHAPTER 4

The Current User/Vendor Mix:
Climate for Groupware Growth?

ROBERT JOHANSEN AND ROBERT MITTMAN

Chapter 2 has presented user views of groupware; Chapter 3 was focused on current vendor product categories from which groupware might grow. Chapter 4 is an inquiry into the connection between user and vendor views of groupware. Is this a climate for groupware growth? Will new product classes have to be created for groupware to become a success?

Table 6 provides a matrix comparison of the 17 user scenarios from Chapter 2 and the 9 current product categories from Chapter 3. If a particular user scenario is beginning to occur within a particular product category, an X is indicated. This does not necessarily mean that current products reflect the user scenario exactly; rather, it means that some activity is beginning to occur in the marketplace. For example, the Telephone Extension scenario fits nicely into the PBX product category, as well as messaging and network services. A few innovative PBX products are appearing with groupware functionality, but this is certainly not in the mainstream of the PBX world. Groupware connections of telephony and messaging are present, but not common. Groupware capabilities can be built into digital conference call bridges, but again such features are just beginning to appear.

In spite of this liberal interpretation of connections, the absence of Xs in Table 6 is apparent. The message is clear: users and vendors are still pretty far apart in their views of groupware. Current product categories do not yet provide many of the groupware functionalities that users are expressing needs for. For vendors, this translates as new product opportunities. For prospective users, it translates the frustrations of searching for or building the right system.

Note: Elliot Gold and Jeff Charles made important contributions to this chapter.

Table 6   COMPARISON OF USER AND VENDOR VIEWS OF GROUPWARE

PRODUCT CATEGORIES

SCENARIOS	Collaborative Systems	Software Extensions	Messaging	LANs	Department Computing	Network Services	PBXs	Add-Ons	Integrated Workstation
1. Facilitation Services	X								
2. Decision Support					X				
3. Telephone Extension			X			X	X		
4. Presentation Prep	X	X							
5. Project Management	X								
6. Calendaring	X	X							
7. Group Writing	X	X		X					
8. Beyond White Board	X							X	
9. Screen Sharing	X	X						X	
10. Computer Conferencing			X	X		X			
11. Text Filtering	X								
12. Teleconference Aid									X
13. Conversational Structuring	X			X					
14. Memory Management	X	X							
15. Spontaneous Interaction						X			
16. Comprehensive Support									X
17. Nonhuman Participants									

The most active connection is the product category called collaborative systems. This is also, however, the least mature of the product categories in the current marketplace—as was clear from our analysis in Chapter 3. Collaborative systems are just starting to happen as real products.

The lack of alignment between user and vendor perspectives does not suggest a climate for immediate groupware growth. But it is important to look for potential development paths from current product classes, even if the connections are not yet drawn. In this chapter we discuss each of the nine current classes in terms of the factors that will enable or inhibit each of them from expanding to include groupware functionalities. After discussing each of the current product categories in this way, we then turn to our assessment of overall forces for and against groupware growth from both a user and a vendor point of view.

COLLABORATIVE/SHARED WORKSPACES

In this category are products that allow the simultaneous sharing of data and graphics from desk to desk, such as Scenario 9 in Chapter 2. Today's products are mostly in the form of PC software that allows two or more users to see the same material on their screens, to modify the contents of files, and to pass control of the files and screen from one person to another. Scenarios 4, 5, 6, 7, 11, 13, and 14 all illustrate various software products that are beginning to occur.

Another type of collaborative or shared workspace is still far from a large-scale market but represents very interesting applications. They are electronic aids in conference rooms (usually in one site, but some in multiple sites with communication capabilities) to support the communications that take place in face-to-face meetings. Scenarios 1 and 8 provide a taste of what such systems might be like.

Enabling Factors

The growth of business teams, as well as other forms of decentralized work groups and project teams, will provide a market pull for suppliers of all types of shared computing products and services. As discussed in Chapter 1, businesses are making increased use of work groups that are spread through the organization, both geographically and in the hierarchy. Examples include large accounting firms that form flexible teams for each large client; manufacturing firms that now involve engineering, assembly, marketing, administration, and even their suppliers in the process of designing new products; and large sales organizations that must pull in repesentatives from several departments to make a sale.

This trend is going to increase in the next few years. The principles of matrix management have become so popular in project-oriented companies that they will continue to spread to the rest of the business world. Growing volatility—including compressed product cycles, takeover threats, episodes like the Tylenol poisonings, and terrorist attacks—will force companies to repond with increasing numbers of task forces, committees, and temporary groups. At the same time, reductions in work forces and efforts to increase productivity will force corporations to make multiple uses of their employees, who will form many groups that reflect their multiple assignments. This trend creates significant market opportunities for suppliers of collaborative systems.

A cadre of pioneering users outside laboratories are now showing the way for user applications. These are users who today have found the limits of single-user PCs. They are appearing as individuals (not always the individuals charged with formal responsibilities for computing activities) and as organizations. For example, one small magazine publisher installed a "homebrew" collaborative system before such systems were on the market. His authors submit articles by modem, and he makes constant use of PCs on the road and in the office. This company has identified many of its needs and has attempted to push the market by calling for others to develop the products and functions it identifies. There are comparable examples from very large user organizations that often have in-house systems expertise to rival that of many vendors.

These users will continue to cobble together systems with their PCs, telephones, fax machines, and modems. Through a very incremental process, they will demonstrate the most economic and usable features and capabilities. It will remain for other companies to seize the opportunity to commercialize these product concepts. These will be the low-end, desk-to-desk applications. The higher-end products will follow a more usual development pattern from laboratory to test market to (developers hope) mass market. The trick will be to distinguish the small (though sometimes profitable) market niches from the more-desirable larger markets.

Today's "substitutes" for computer communication—mailing lists, routing slips, rekeying, telephone tag, mailing of diskettes—are so inefficient that a market imperative for better communication exists. That market imperative is being tackled in bits and pieces for products such as document readers, offshore rekeying of masses of data, and voice mail. Together, the pieces make up some of the constituent parts of the technology for groupware. They have not yet combined to make a climate in which people actively think about communicating through computers as a priority, but once enough pieces are in place, the markets will develop.

In the academic community, interest in the use of computers as communication tools is growing. As discussed in Chapter 1, research conferences on this topic are becoming increasingly common. Publications such as the Association of Computing Machinery's *Transactions on Office Information Systems* (New York City) and other professional journals are now beginning to treat the subject.

Academic activity translates, eventually, into products and markets—whether more or less quickly depending on the specific groups and technology involved. Funding agencies from government and business provide one of the most fundamental pushes, but faculty members also exert a good deal of control over the course of their research. Many of their graduate students now end up working in business where, acting as entrepreneurs (or as intrapreneurs), they can translate their graduate school research interests into marketable products.

The first user organization to adopt technology often gains a competitive advantage over organizations that are slower to adapt. This clearly has been the case with information and communication technologies such as computer-based airline reservation systems and hospital supply ordering systems. The message that computers can provide a competitive advantage is "in the air" as an incentive for people considering collaborative systems.

Inhibiting Factors

"Big companies can't make money selling conceptual change."[1] This is a general concern for vendors, but it applies most to new categories of groupware products, such as what we are calling collaborative systems. The dominant concept of a meeting in most corporations is not primarily one of collaboration. People use meetings to move information, to gain political consensus, or even to perpetuate adversarial roles. More importantly, people are not used to "meeting" via computer. The question with collaborative systems is not whether they do what they advertise, but whether what they do is perceived to have value by user organizations. It will take a cultural shift that most companies are not willing (or even able) to make unless the payoff is large and very visible. The collaborative systems of today are unlikely to prompt that perceptual shift quickly.

A down-to-earth measure of the magnitude of conceptual change involved in a new product is how long it takes to explain the idea to the uninitiated. For collaborative systems, it takes a long time.

Very few products that came directly from the technologist's bench to the store shelf have ever sold in quantity. In particular, products that generate a lot of excitement among technologists tend to be those that solve technologists' problems, not necessarily the problems of business and industry. For many collaborative systems this is the case. Most of the systems are not only at the experimental stage; they are also designed for use in laboratories.

With the exception of a few pioneering users, there has been little expressed market demand for collaborative systems. Much of the activity in technologies that could be a basis for collaborative systems is centered in noncollaborative uses; for example, LANs are being justified and used because they allow the sharing of individual resources such as laser printers, not because they enable overt collaboration.

Many collaborative systems are so complex that only sophisticated users can operate them. This, in part, is a reflection of developing products that serve the needs of the technologists who develop them. The basic concepts used in shared systems—passing a baton, shared spaces, changing modes of work—are acts that we all perform in person very instinctively. But it is only a sophisticated person who has the interest and ability to invest the time and effort it takes to make the instinctive explicit.

Of course, simpler products exist that individually make up some of the parts of collaborative systems. Electronic copyboards that simply make paper copies of writing from white boards or flip-chart pads are such an example. Individually, these products are more accessible to the average user. In proportion to their perceived utility (modified by a factor for marketing expertise), they will find a market.

In addition, several other factors will influence the development of collaborative systems: (1) The lack of technical and organizational infrastructures for computer-supported groups is an obvious problem. (2) The "bunker mentality" in the computer industry may persist as computer companies struggle to show favorable short-term financial results. The competitive diversity of interests among vendors will distort the incentives so that orchestrated actions for new product concepts will be lacking. Vendors may settle for a known share of an existing pie rather than face the risks of expanding the pie. (3) The slow development of voice recognition and other easy interfaces will inhibit acceptance of computer-assisted communication among executives; only the keyboard literate will use the technologies.

In sum, the market for collaborative systems will remain quite fragmented in the near term, with many independent efforts and some successes, but without a unifying theme or product. Some technologies such as hardcopy white boards will be incorporated into conference rooms, but few integrated rooms will be sold during the next few years.

Similarly, a number of PC-oriented software products for sharing screens and other collaborative functions are already selling in modest numbers. None will find mass markets right away, but there will be real success stories.

This is not to say that the longer-term outlook for collaborative systems is weak. The underlying trends—particularly the growth of decentralized work groups and project teams—are real and are moving in the right direction. But it will take time for business to accomplish the conceptual change required to adopt these systems more widely. Meanwhile, small companies will find profitable niches for products and services. Also, a few large companies will use such systems to achieve substantial competitive advantages.

SOFTWARE EXTENSIONS

Groupware can be added to existing software as a new feature, bypassing the barriers of selling the concept usually associated with more direct approaches to collaborative systems. Such applications are illustrated by Scenarios 4, 6, 7, 9, and 14 in Chapter 2.

Enabling Factors

Software sells. Almost overnight, a sales infrastructure has been created to sell software to a wide variety of customer groups. There are also existing product categories that customers understand well: word processing, spreadsheets, database programs, communications packages, graphics packages, and so on. The existence of this sales infrastructure and the established product categories provide a major enabler for this approach to groupware introduction.

Although software is selling, the software providers need ever-increasing revenues to sustain that growth. Everyone is looking for winners; the search is constant, and the search is intense. This drive for new ideas creates on openness to concepts like groupware.

Groupware, of course, inherently means multiple users. To software providers, it means multiple sales. If a group decides to go with a particular groupware product, all the group members get copies of the software. A single sale is really a multiple sale. Vendors like this.

Moreover, some of the existing software categories are getting stale. How many new features can you add to a word processor or a spreadsheet? In the constant quest for newness, groupware features can provide a new set of sizzles.

Inhibiting Factors

Although it is attractive to sell "at the margins," where a new idea gets sold as a feature rather than a completely new idea, there are also potential downsides to consider. For example, selling features may mean little or no new revenue for the software provider. Certainly, a vendor has trouble charging as much for a new feature as for a new product. This can be an inhibitor, unless positioning and pricing structures can be created to make the introduction of groupware features profitable for the providers.

Groupware functions can be quite difficult to add onto existing products. In conventional software, only one user has access to a file at a time. Groupware confuses that relationship, as many users may work on a file. Further, in some groupware products, an "audit trail" of who made what changes must be kept. All of these factors add to the difficulty and cost of extending software to include groupware functions.

Software developers typically add to their products in response to the interests and requests of existing users. Developers will put primary effort into meeting those needs. Features like groupware may take a lower priority on development agendas, unless expressed user interest is high.

ELECTRONIC MESSAGING PRODUCTS AND SERVICES

Three main forms of messaging are included here: electronic mail, computer conferencing, and voice mail. These all are positioned as alternatives to other forms of communication—electronic mail for paper mail, computer conferencing for meetings, voice mail for telephone. Each of them also adds new dimensions to communication and exposes some of the attractive features of people communicating through computers. In Chapter 2, Scenario 10 provides a taste of computer conferencing, which is the most unusual product type in this class, but also the most directly connected to groupware. Scenario 3, the Telephone Extension, includes voice mail capabilities.

Enabling Factors

Many existing competitors for electronic messaging have demonstrated performance problems—the U.S. Postal Service is infamous for delays; the cost of delivering a letter by messenger can exceed the potential benefit of sending the letter; telephone tag can delay a short conversation for days; a face-to-face meeting often is a costly way to resolve simple problems; express delivery is dependable but expensive.

The electronic substitutes offer significant advantages in many cases. Electronic mail is fast and relatively inexpensive. Voice mail certainly cuts down on telephone tag. Computer conferences allow groups to communicate across time and space barriers. Fax machines provide instantaneous transmission of printed documents and PC-to-fax links close the loop between printed and electronic documents.

One problem that has plagued most new computer communication technologies is the absence of standards. In particular, an application like electronic mail, which requires compatibility between systems if it is to work, needs standards or some form of interconnection process. The promulgation by the international standards body CCITT of what is called the X.400 standard is the type of sign users are waiting for to make purchases. By itself, it may not be a sufficient condition to fire market acceptance, but it is a necessary prerequisite for many corporate buyers. The decision to incorporate electronic mail into a computer system or to buy a system with an electronic mail feature will be far easier with standards.

For many corporate users of computer systems, signing up for a computer conferencing or electronic mail system outside the corporation is simply too much effort. Particularly for low-level users, getting authorization to subscribe can entail burdensome bureaucratic steps. Increasingly, those corporations that allow participation in commercial electronic mail and conferencing systems will provide gateways to their networks. Easy access will speed the acceptance and use of messaging.

Inhibiting Factors

Potential users of messaging technologies react the way many potential users of almost every new technology—from stone to steam to silicon—have: "I'm doing fine just the way I am." The same is true with electronic messaging. People are quite comfortable using meetings, mail, and the telephone. And even when they complain vocally (as they do about telephone tag), they perceive that the electronic alternative is too complicated to use, so they may not let the salesperson in the door. The "keyboard generation" of managers is still rising in the ranks, and thus electronic mail and computer conferencing will continue to encounter barriers in the short run.

Overnight delivery services provide an alternative to messaging that both managers and secretaries find easy to use. Such services have the important advantage of conforming to the existing scheme of document preparation and handling: the executive drafts or dictates; the secretary polishes, seals, and addresses; someone else (a live and usually friendly human) does the rest. Importantly, the package is still sealed when it reaches the recipient, who can usually tell if the message has been seen or tampered with. The cost of these services, although high for routine correspondence, is still below the pain threshold for most businesses.

International messaging standards are encouraging, but still problematic. Widespread implementation is bound to move slowly. Meanwhile, system designers must use some standard. The proliferation of message standards may make it as difficult to send a message between systems as it is to fit a Whitworth bolt with a metric wrench.

The large number of messaging networks, combined with a still small subscriber base, makes it difficult to find a critical mass for communication. The implementation of a national subscriber directory is helping. Still, it is hard to reach people on other systems. Other inhibiting factors include: (1) The current low subscriber base lends a self-limiting dynamic to electronic mail and computer conferencing. Why bother using it if you can't reach the people you want to reach? (2) A persistent lack of an installed base of terminal devices (in comparison to telephones) makes it impossible to appeal to a significant part of the population. (3) High start-up costs for interface equipment and software licensing make voice mail a difficult sell to most businesses. (4) Telephone answering machines spoil the soup for voice mail in two ways: the low quality of the latter's early machines soured some potential users on the idea; other users already have adequate machines and feel they do not need the next generation.

Although the poor performance of many conventional messaging methods—mail, telephone, and messengers—appears to create an attractive opportunity for vendors of electronic messaging, these markets have been surprisingly slow to develop.

Of the three messaging technologies mentioned above, the prospects for voice mail are the best. It is a technology that can be installed centrally but functions through the universal terminal—the telephone. Its functions are clear to most users right away, and it is relatively easy to use. Most important, it can be circumvented easily, so that users have a familiar alternative (a human operator) if they want it.

Electronic mail has the next-brightest prospects. Conceiving of the technology as a way for white-collar workers to communicate directly unnecessarily limits the scope of the market. If the technology waits for white-collar workers to become comfortable with keyboards and otherwise change their behavior patterns, it will have a slow growth. If, like Federal Express, it becomes another way for secretaries to move messages, its use will increase much more rapidly.

Computer conferencing is the least likely to develop quickly, because it requires a real change in behavior for users. Keyboard proficiency and the patience to move at slower than real time, for example, are required. Targeted applications will certainly be profitable in the short run, but the concept by itself will be hard to sell. As one disgruntled president of a failing computer-conferencing company told us: "In the last two years, I've proved that you can't sell something called computer conferencing."

In sum, user inertia is a persistent force, despite the obvious inefficiencies of the status quo. This new industry has spent 15 years in a very gradual takeoff stage. The proliferation of messaging options such as automatic log-on software and gateways to messaging systems indicates that the market may be finally taking off with some vigor. This may be one of the technologies in which there is a tendency to overrate the potential in the short run and to underrate it in the long run.

To the extent that these technologies are introduced into user organizations to soothe perceived pain, some of the additional advantages of people communicating through computers will be introduced through the back door. For example, electronic mail makes the broadcast of printed messages to selected mailboxes easy; this is a form of electronic publishing. Computer conferencing is a good facilitator of team project work. Voice mail adds editing capabilities as well as providing some of the same advantages of electronic mail. These additional functions could pave the way for acceptance of groupware additions to messaging systems.

LOCAL AREA NETWORKS

LANs are already present in many organizations and are fulfilling their primary purposes—giving computer users access to shared resources such as file servers, communication ports, and printers. It is the secondary purpose—the extent to which these technologies will play a part in people communicating through computers—that is of interest here. LANs could provide a solid infrastructure for the development of groupware. Scenario 16 in Chapter 2 provides a taste of the integration benefits offered to users by LANs.

Enabling Factors

LANs have very healthy growth prospects independent of any groupware applications. They are most often installed as a way of sharing expensive resources like hard disks and laser printers. It is these base functions that will get LANs into businesses. Once they are there, groupware applications can be developed incrementally.

Some of the features of LANs translate directly into groupware. For example, some have electronic mail functions built in. Increasing use of LANs has forced developers to make LAN versions of their software. These versions must cope with some of the key issues in groupware—file control and resolution of conflicts among users. Further, it acclimates the vendors to using site and multiple-user licenses.

Growing standardization of LANs is removing some of the uncertainty that potential buyers face. This makes LANs a more attractive hardware option.

Inhibiting Factors

The cost to wire a LAN in anything but new construction is quite high. This cost has been, and will continue to be, a brake on overall LAN sales. Almost every office has a telephone line leading into it. That wire can be a formidable LAN competitor if the cost of a terminal device that converts the telephone line for simultaneous voice and data use is less than the cost of running a new data line.

DEPARTMENTAL COMPUTING

Departmental computing provides shared computing support for groups of end users, typically within a particular part of an organization. The question is whether these shared computing resources can be steered toward inclusion of groupware functionalities.

Enabling Factors

Considerable momentum exists for establishing and maintaining departmental computing environments. This momentum has been created independently from the move toward groupware. In fact, many departmental computing environments have users that do no or very little actual collaborative work through the system. Now that these environments are in place, however, they provide natural and very attractive pathways for groupware products and services.

The creation of such pathways is critical for groupware to succeed. Most groupware products assume the existence of a telecommunications infrastructure, but this infrastructure is often either absent or deficient. Departmental computing solves the infrastructure problems convincingly.

Technology trends are supporting the emergence of departmental computing. PCs are beginning to have the power to handle groups of users and the software to handle them gracefully. Large mainframe computers are no longer necessary for many types of computer support.

The trend toward decentralized organizations and business teams, discussed in Chapter 1, provides further enabling forces for departmental computing to develop as a major home for groupware.

Inhibiting Factors

In a real sense, it is much easier to provide a routine shared computing resource than it is to support collaboration through those computers. Group collaboration is inherently messy; it involves lots of organizational, sociological, and psychological dynamics. Many people who created departmental computing environments will prefer to avoid the mess, to keep themselves at arm's length from the services they provide to users. Also, the skills needed to operate a successful departmental computing operation are likely to be different from those needed to provide successful groupware services.

For groupware to be attractive for departmental computing providers, there must be incentives. These incentives are not yet clear. Will users find departmental computing more attractive if groupware services are available through the system? Are there advantages to the system operators, as well as the users? Until these questions can be answered persuasively, there will be no driving force for groupware via departmental computers.

The match between departmental computing and groupware, however, looks like a natural. It will just take time and experience to spell out the opportunities, the advantages, and the specific ways of making it happen.

NETWORK SERVICES

Network-based services include enhanced telephone services provided by the long-haul carriers and local telephone companies, gateway services through the network, and certain bypass opportunities. These services will make use of media such as fiber optics, satellite, and private microwave networks. The exact medium, though, is not as important as the way the service provides group support. Scenario

3 in Chapter 2 describes how the telephone network can be used to provide various forms of groupware services.

Enabling Factors

The ubiquity of the telephone network makes it attractive as a medium for groupware. User inertia, the habit of using the telephone system as the primary means of communication, will benefit the development of network-based services in data, graphics, image, and in some cases, video. If people think of groupware as more of a communication task than a computing task, the telephone network is likely to be the medium of choice.

Additionally, the relative technical ease with which one can add services and features centrally makes the economies of scale in the network attractive. If regulators allow it, there is no lower cost way to implement voice mail, computer conferencing, electronic mail, and most other forms of computer communication than through the computers that are already part of the telephone network.

The ease of use of the telephone system makes it attractive to most users and potential users. If user interfaces can be built that lead a user step by step into more sophisticated applications, then telephone companies have a very strong position from the start.

Voice and data bridges will enhance network-based services by providing not only multiple functionality, but also much flexibility to the network. (Such bridges provide conference telephone calls, plus display of data to multiple sites.) Today's voice/data bridges are still somewhat limited in terms of their ability to handle multiple data requirements elegantly. But as the bridges themselves grow in sophistication and features (especially handling image data), so can network services that provide access to the bridges.

Other enabling factors include: (1) An abundance of optical fiber will make long-haul high-speed data and bandwidth so inexpensive that the transport component of costs will be far less important. (2) The regional Bell operating companies' eagerness for new telecommunications standards such as ISDN pushes them to adopt and distribute technologies and services that promote people communicating through computers. (3) A more-flexible menu of services (ultimately, bandwidth on demand) makes the network a more attractive place for users.

Inhibiting Factors

Regulation of the communications industry, and in particular the competitive politics of offering new services, will continue to act as a brake for providers of new network services. Local telephone companies in particular will face much resistance to their efforts to move into value-added information services. Although the overall trend is still toward liberalization of lines of business, it is not implausible that the brakes could be put on before the local telephone companies move into these areas.

Some of the regulatory issues that may restrain development of network-based services include protection of new markets from large competitors, renewed lines of business restrictions in response to some recent diversification advantages, and protection of consumers from the capital costs of implementing ISDN.

Competition in long-haul voice communications could hold back innovative network-based services such as ISDN while the common carriers battle it out over prices instead of features. Price cuts in voice communications require lower costs in operations, and they would not allow high-cost start-up ventures for markets of unknown sizes. Meanwhile, the technical complexity of ISDN is daunting. Several trials of pieces of the technology are under way, but no conclusive results are in yet. ISDN is much more a vision (actually visions) than it is an actual service. Like many other technological holy grails, ISDN may become somewhat of a joke in the end, or at least a disappointment. Skeptics in the user world have speculated that ISDN (to telecommunications companies) stands for "I see dollars now."

Other inhibiting factors include: (1) The network, although providing excellent access between sites, sometimes does not work as well within a single site. It fails to compete effectively in the single-site, small-work-group market. Local-area work groups are very important as a potential market, however. (2) Alternative network connections are justified in user organizations as being a less expensive way to provide the same level of communications service rather than as a way to provide higher value-added services.

The telephone network is in a unique position in terms of technological appropriateness and market strength to dominate many aspects of the groupware market. The fact that almost all communication that is not on paper goes through some part of the telephone network assures at least a passive role for the regional Bell operating companies and the long-distance carriers. But they could play a much larger role. This role could include on-network voice mail with advanced message storage, retrieval and archiving; simultaneous transmission of voice and data on a single phone line; and even computer resources on demand. Long-haul network providers have already experimented with aspects of communication through computers, including AT&T's Alliance conference calling bridge and GTE's Telenet packet-switched network.

Two strong factors make it unlikely that the regional Bell operating companies will assume a dominant role in the next five years. First, they remain tied by restrictions on the lines of business they can enter. These restrictions, though in the process of falling, may be more robust than most observers assume. A movement to renew line of business restrictions on the regional Bells could emerge not only from concerns over unfair dominance of infant markets, but also from their demonstrated proclivity to lose money in risky ventures.

This last point leads to the second factor, which affects all carriers. There is not yet a clear groupware market for network providers to enter, let alone dominate. They have not yet shown the marketing prowess required to create a new market. The best bet for the carriers will be to form alliances with smaller partners who can point the way to profitable segments and lay the groundwork for large-scale efforts.

PRIVATE BRANCH EXCHANGE

PBXs form the core of the voice communication in many medium and large companies. As such, they can also form the core of groupware functions. Scenario 3 in Chapter 2 explores this possibility.

Enabling Factors

PBXs connect the most-accessible groupware terminal—the telephone. To the extent that groupware functions are available through PBXs, many people will have access to them. This vision of groupware benefits from the ease of using the telephone for most communication.

Stiff competition in the PBX market will encourage competition on features, including some that facilitate groupware uses. Some of the added features will include voice mail, the easy addition of more powerful or versatile computing functions, more-capable terminals, and multiplexed voice and data. This increase in functionality in a single package will give PBXs a stronger position in the market.

Though there is a technological push in PBXs to provide sophisticated, high-data-rate features, most groupware applications can use voice-grade lines. These applications, such as file transfers and electronic mail, do not require more capacity than that offered by voice-grade lines. Future applications, such as images and photographs, may require higher bandwidth.

PBXs can make their best contributions by expanding to data traffic the features they do best for voice. These are control, restriction, routing, and scheduling. Applications for groupware include accounting for data calls, providing easily accessible links to packet networks, and scheduling off-hour data exchanges. Enhanced features might include compatibility with existing PC communications packages and value-added features such as site-licensed software.

Inhibiting Factors

Users face considerable uncertainty. On the product side, they cannot know whether to look to PBXs or to LANs to become the most developed and supported to meet their computer communications needs. Within their organizations, their managers are uncertain about the future (and even existing) mix of voice and data traffic, the demand for high-speed data, the type of terminal equipment, and even the number of terminals. In an environment of uncertainty, users tend to wait and see what develops.

Faced with uncertainty, users may experiment with small investments to keep up with some of the latest developments in technologies that interest them. They are much less likely to make the heavy capital investment that enhanced PBXs require. We return again to the scenario of the cobbled-together system that grows higgledly-piggledly as the needs of the organization grow. This scenario fits the small- to mid-sized organization; larger organizations with more leeway in their budgets can affort to hire the expertise needed to make an informed decision on their voice and data communications requirements.

In an environment in which cost control is important, the enabling factor of competition on features of PBXs may be undermined by a need to keep costs low. Manufacturers may hold back existing technological developments from the marketplace to keep prices low. Under that type of regime, the features most likely to be dropped are those that extend the scope of the product the most. Thus, many of the technologies that support people communicating through computers may be delayed in favor of features that concentrate on enhancing voice service.

The prospect of ISDN means that much more information can be sent over standard telephone lines. This prospect is causing a wait-and-see attitude among uses who would rather buy the state of the art as a service from a local telephone company than invest in equipment that may soon be obsolete.

ADD-ON AND PERIPHERAL DEVICES

This product category includes PC add-on boards and peripheral devices that can "beef up" the plain PC to make it a more effective tool for communication. Graphics boards, external cameras, voice digitizers, and image processors are all part of the technology. More fundamentally, modems are an integral part of any communicating computer. Certain peripherals, such as large external storage devices, can support communication through computers as well as other activities. Scenarios 8 and 9 in Chapter 2 provide examples of how such add-ons might be used.

Enabling Factors

High-resolution graphics boards and monitors are among the best-selling PC add-ons today and are growing rapidly in capabilities and sales. At the initial stages, a large part of this market was to satisfy the desire of IBM and compatible PC users to have text as clear as that produced by the Apple Macintosh. At the same time, graphics (conventionally prepared) are one of the mainstays of conference room communication. Many users, once exposed to the graphics capability of their PCs, use computer-prepared graphics extensively (as in Scenario 4 in Chapter 2). It is a natural step from here to the use of shared graphics screens and to higher-quality images.

Alliances are now being formed between small entrepreneurs making add-ons and peripherals and large vendors with greater marketing muscle. The alliances are helping smaller companies to find large markets and big companies to find new products or services. These alliances are expanding the market. A classic example is Optel Communications Inc. (New York City), a small manufacturer of PC add-on boards and software. Optel is working with AT&T Communications. The smaller company makes graphic communication tools; it adds interactive graphics to PCs through an expansion board and software, allowing users to communicate in voice and graphics over a single telephone line. AT&T is looking to stimulate demand for its Alliance audio and graphic teleconferencing service, but it needs terminal products to demonstrate the features of Alliance. Through joint marketing, Optel has improved its sales, and AT&T is winning new customers for its teleconferencing service, customers who also use AT&T's telephone network for long-distance tolls, where the bigger profits are. We expect to see more of these relationships that bring the marketing muscle of the larger companies to stimulate sales by the smaller makers of add-ons and peripherals.

The present surge in interest in desktop publishing will have a beneficial effect on many other parts of the PC market. Many organizations are buying PCs equipped with high-resolution graphics, large memory capacity, external storage, document and image scanners, digitizing pads, and laser printers to do in-house desktop publishing. This application has captured the imagination of U.S. corporations. Users are being exposed to the capabilities of fully loaded machines, the effectiveness of text and graphics documents, and the concept of communicating documents. This can only benefit the prospects for groupware.

Several other enabling factors could have an effect, including: (1) A higher market penetration of modems on PCs allows more desktops to be addressed and accessed by users currently proficient in computer communications skills. This will begin to provide the connectivity required for increased use of groupware. (2) The cost of PC add-ons is low relative to the initial threshold costs of integrated voice/data workstations. Users can now build their PCs into special-purpose workstations economically, adding only those features they need for through low-cost add-on peripherals. (3) The amount of remote work, including telecommuting, is growing. Slow as it is, there is a very gradual trend toward working from home and operating entire cottage businesses from homes. In the short run, remote work will mean communication from geographically separated company sites.

Inhibiting Factors

The task of fully configuring a PC with graphics, scanners, image digitizers, voice digitizers, and even cameras is a daunting one. Making all the right wiring connections, configuring the software, setting switches on the boards, making sure the right disks are available—these are all too difficult for the average user. Some sophisticated users will balk at the amount of work required. In fact, the equipment needed to configure a PC is often not fully compatible, advertising brochures not withstanding.

These problems will mean that the primary audience for built-up communicating computers will fall into two groups. One group—early adopters and pioneering users—understands and appreciates the use of communicating computers. But many people in that group, especially those from the engineering culture found in many companies, suffer from the "not invented here" syndrome and resist replacing the gems they've cobbled together. A second group—corporate information centers—also has the ability to set the machines up, but it responds largely to the needs of users in the organization, who may not yet be able to visualize what a loaded PC could do for them. This corporate impasse will be difficult to break. There is a definite opportunity here for providers who package easy-to-use systems, even if they have limited functionality and high price tags.

All that has been said about installation (usually attempted only by the sophisticated user) goes double for the use of the systems. Even simple communications between PCs require a good deal of sophistication. Log-on codes must be remembered, the right disk must be in the right place at the right time, actions must be done in the right sequence and synchronized. The more equipment in a system, the more likely it is that some of it will break down. Changes in software that seem obvious to experienced users can utterly frustrate a less-experienced user. And it takes only a few such frustrations to turn that user off permanently.

Some of the early systems have been extremely complex to use and difficult to demonstrate to new and prospective users alike. This has tended to put up a barrier to purchasing new, easier-to-use systems, as the potential user has a distrust of such marketing euphemisms as "easy-to-use," "end user computing," and "user friendly." Some of these ill-conceived efforts will do more to reinforce user inertia than to replace it.

Other inhibiting factors include: (1) Evolution of the underlying hardware base makes it hard for suppliers of add-ons to keep current. (2) Concerns for security are not resolved, and encryption is expensive and not widely sold.

Add-ons and peripherals are a promising source of hardware for people communicating through computers. The large, installed base of PCs ensures that vendors will continue to develop innovative add-ons. On the high end, the demand created by desktop publishing and other hardware-intensive applications will mean an increased base of very capable computers in the field. On the low end, the incremental nature of the investment in additional capabilities will allow more users to justify the equipment needed to get minimal communication through their computers and later to enhance it.

Many of the add-ons add greatly to the versatility of the PC. But in many cases, the versatility of the PC will never be exploited. The communication capabilities will be seen as secondary, as serving some other primary objective (for example, publishing a newsletter). Users may keep a narrow perspective on the capabilities of their machines. Thus, a marketing effort to users of certain add-ons may be required to get them to use the communication capacity of their machines fully even after they buy them.

This increased hardware base is a strong positive factor for the spread of groupware. But the preference for discrete applications will make that market fragmentary. Add-ons for specific groupware applications will be very promising, however, as long as they can be made into products in a way that is attractive to prospective customers.

INTEGRATED WORKSTATIONS

Integrated voice and data workstations are a class of products that combine many of the functions of the fully loaded PC with the telephone into a single box on a worker's desk. Such systems range in complexity from a terminal plus telephone dialer to a fully integrated package that incorporates voice, data, graphics, mainframe access, and even speech synthesis. Scenario 16 in Chapter 2 describes such a user application for groupware.

Enabling Factors

Users have a natural interest in integrating both the work they do with computers and the computer tools they use. Current use frustrations about incompatible systems and components are high. Users find that the pieces of their system often do not fit, particularly if more than one vendor is involved. The rhetoric of compatibility is wearing thin, as users find that the responsibility for details is often left on their shoulders. Groupware functionalities would be much more attractive if users did not have to worry about the hassles of interconnection.

Integration is also attractive at the physical level: there is only so much room on a desktop. Integrated workstations have a smaller "footprint" than the space taken up by stand-alone components. Integration reduces the clutter.

Inhibiting Factors

The long list of integrated workstation failures and the short list of actual successes scare off both vendors and users. Some providers saw workstations as having so much added value that they could demand premium prices for them. A series of products from a range of vendors has been offered at between 50 and 100 percent over the price of PCs; enough, we believe, to have limited demand. Other "executive" workstations have been priced even higher, and they have not been sold very often. Such high prices have turned off potential buyers, in a market where even the inexpensive systems have been hard to sell.

User organizations respond to perceived needs among their users. It has been, and will continue to be, difficult to show that integrated workstations fill a demonstrated need. All integrated systems must fight the natural incrementalism that is built into the planning and acquisitions of most organizations. It is easier (once the camel's nose—the PC—is under the tent) to justify a graphics board or an autodialer than it is to justify a whole new package all at once.

Other inhibiting factors include: (1) The technology for voice recognition and understanding (the one feature that might convince many executives of the value of an integrated workstation on their desks) is slow to develop. (2) Competition from PCs loaded with add-ons that simulate workstations are more flexible, less expensive, and easier to improve than most integrated systems. They steal the march. (3) User companies have standards, usually around a single vendor. Other stations can, integrated or not, have a tough time in that kind of market.

We are pessimistic about stand-alone integrated workstations, particularly if they have closed architectures. Such products are very hard to sell in the current climate, and we do not expect this to change easily or quickly.

There is an interesting wild card development, however, which is best illustrated by a company called Metaphor Computer Systems (Mountain View, California). Metaphor was formed by several leading figures at Xerox, including people from both marketing and software engineering. The engineers were lead designers of the Xerox Star workstation; one, Charles Irbe, is also on alumnus of Doug Engelbart's pioneering laboratory, discussed in Chapter 1. This background is revealed in Metaphor's design: windows, icons, mouse, keypad, and so on. The system is targeted specifically toward sales and marketing operations in packaged-goods industries.

Using Metaphor requires a major user commitment in both Metaphor equipment and internal support. For the system to be useful, an internal infrastructure must be created to feed in sales, competitors' sales, and other data needed by the Metaphor users. Our assessment is that Metaphor is very good at providing their side of the bargain. It remains to be seen if there are users out there who can provide the other side to create successful user applications. If they can, Metaphor (or other competing) workstations could have at least a niche in the marketplace. This is a big if, however. For the moment, Metaphor is a bellwether company to watch. It has become profitable, and it may signal a workable approach to the voice/data workstations angle on groupware.

FORCES FOR AND AGAINST GROUPWARE

In addition to the market dynamics of current products described previously, groupware vendors will encounter general forces for and against groupware. Table 7 summarizes the overall forces we see from a vendor point of view.

Vendors are always searching for new products, but the need is particularly pressing right now. This is a quest for the "next Lotus 1-2-3," and it is a burning quest in Silicon Valley, the Boston/Cambridge area, and other areas of software creativity.

The pursuit of group-oriented products is reflective of the fact that most prospective providers have a strong personal realization of the value of teamwork. Indeed, many vendors make heavy use of teams in their own work; for example, ad hoc teams are a way of life in Silicon Valley. Thus, groupware is a class of products for which many vendors have not only acceptance, but also firsthand understanding.

Another positive force for vendors is the existence of building blocks for groupware such as PCs, private networks, and audio conference calling through digital bridges. Although assembling these building blocks is not always easy, their very existence indicates a potential leveraging effect for new groupware products.

Finally, current groupware research is a fueling factor for vendors. This research is occurring at places like Xerox's PARC and the Microelectronics and Computer Corporation (MCC) in Austin, for example. In addition, many university efforts are under way at places like MIT, NYU, Harvard, Claremont, the University of Arizona, the University of Michigan, Brown, and Stanford. Such efforts provide fertile ground for upstream product ideas and specific seed efforts that vendors can pursue.

On the negative side of the ledger in Table 7, we again see the tricky "what is it?" question regarding groupware. Positioning and packaging are key for vendors as well as users. Users are expecting vendors to do more than simply offer a technology; they want clear-

Table 7   Vendor Forces for and against Groupware

For	Against
A major search for new products is under way	It is hard to define and position groupware
Vendors realize the importance of group work	It is hard to find quick hits
There are useful "building blocks" in the market	Developing group software is logistically difficult
Promising R&D activities are under way	Users have no incentives to share success stories

cut applications. And, if early experience with groupware is any clue, it will not be easy to find quick hits. Major success will probably take considerable nurturing.

A third barrier to computer-supported groups is even more down to earth: group-oriented software is not easy to develop. Most of the problems are nitty-gritty (for example, keeping track of multiple users), rather than state-of-the-art technological.[2] The growth of group-oriented software will be tempered by the practical difficulties of creating this software. The transition from individual to group software is a major transition, and designers will have much to learn in the new world of group support.

Finally, there are few success stories to date regarding computer-supported teams. The 17 approaches described in Chapter 1 provide a good taste for the present range of activities, but practical user experience is limited. Most of the approaches are not fully tested by users. There are incentives not to exchange success stories with other users when they do occur. Because work teams often are engaged in important tasks, sensitivities crop up regarding competitive advantage. Indeed, the current groupware users we interviewed for this book often allowed us to discuss only general characteristics of their applications, because of concerns about competitive advantage. Further, it is not clear that the successes of the first teams to use groupware (often within developers' organizations) will translate to the general business environment.

Product groups in the major computer manufacturers (as compared to upstream R&D groups within those same companies) are not yet interested in group-oriented products. This is understandable. For most vendors, particularly in these days of short-term financial pressures, little interest exists in products that require customers to make conceptual changes. At this point, R&D groups at major vendors are pursuing group-oriented products, but the transfer has not been made to the product planners. This transfer is occurring, but how long will it take?

In addition to current products and vendor dynamics, there are other forces that will shape the overall user climate for groupware growth. Table 8 summarizes these forces, from a user point of view.

First, and probably most important, is the general trend toward business teams. As discussed in Chapter 1, teams have become the order of the day for many large companies. Cross-organizational groups are the most common: project teams or task forces that have important mandates and tight deadlines. These groups are searching

Table 8   User Forces for and against Groupware

For	Against
Popularity of business teams and naturalness of group work	Poor packaging and positioning of groupware products
Acceptance of computers for competitive advantage	Need for conceptual sell to prospective users
Penetration of PCs	Poor links to existing products and infrastructure
Penetration of LANs, private networks, and public network services	Dependence on small vendors

for tools that will help them get their jobs done. Computer support often seems to provide an answer, or at least part of an answer. Most business teams also have access to funding for such computer tools. A purchase by a business team will be evaluated by different criteria than a purchase made by a data-processing, MIS, or telecommunications manager. Whereas operational people typically are worried about saving money, business teams often are focusing on ways to make money. Consequently, the latter often will be more willing to try something new and to take promising risks.

As a side benefit, measuring the performance of business teams is often more tractable than measuring the performance of large organizations or individuals. If a team has a clear task and a timetable, its productivity should be measurable—or at least more measurable. This measurability of effects should make business teams even more attractive to executives. Business teams may use groupware to enhance and document their performance.

Second, but still very important, is the acceptance by most businesses that computers can be used to gain competitive advantages. This notion has been promoted by the good business schools for over five years, but now it is finally having an effect on the masses of U.S. business people. Because of this realization, there should be more receptivity toward the idea of computer-supported teams or other related concepts.

Third, the penetration of PCs has now grown to the point at which interconnection of team members at their desks is usually practical. The evolution of business-oriented software supports this trend. All those PCs sitting on desks, even if they are not being used, represent potential building blocks for equipping computer-supported teams. Many business people also seem to have a sense that their companies might have moved too quickly in the race from the mainframe to the isolated desktop. Users often realize that they want their PCs to be linked at least to the computers of their closest co-workers. Fueling this trend is the increasing popularity of LANs.

The penetration of PCs parallels the penetration of LANs and other forms of private telecommunications networks. The growing popularity of such networks is providing a potential infrastructure for groupware communications. With an accepted linkage among users in place, the introduction of groupware becomes much easier. In addition to private networks, public telecommunications networks are also providing an increasing range of services and options for groupware connections. Such services will be particularly important not only for smaller user organizations that do not have the resources to construct private networks, but also for large users who opt against a "build your own" option.

On the opposite side of the ledger in Table 8, we list forces that are working against groupware, or at least make it a hard sell. The first two items combine to form the biggest current groupware block. These items are also related to the "what to call it" problem discussed in Chapter 1. Groupware is a foreign concept to most users. To be attractive, it must be defined in terms of their needs and be packaged so that it can be internally understood and its cost justified. Current products do not stack up well by such criteria. Indeed, groupware products as currently positioned seem destined to remake the mistakes that teleconferencing and other new information systems have already made. (See Appendix A for details on relevant experiences from the teleconferencing marketplace.)

Beyond product positioning and packaging, there are nitty-gritty problems of connecting groupware products to existing software. For example, some group writing or group brainstorming packages are incompatible with existing word-processing systems. Such annoyances are frequent in the new world of groupware, and they block large-scale expansion beyond the early adopters who are willing to put up with such things.

Also, for those organizations that have not established their own private networks or relationships with public networks, there are often problems in getting groupware users connected to each other. Groupware needs to be able to blend in well with existing infrastructures for communications.

Finally, the current groupware marketplace is dominated by innovative, small vendors. Such companies are often long on creativity and short on stability. This makes users nervous, particularly about large purchases from companies that could disappear at any moment.

The overall prospects for groupware growth are promising, in spite of the substantial inhibitors. Users are demonstrating significant interest in group communication through computers. Some of the hardware building blocks are in place. Much software development remains to be done, and not all of the incentives are in place for that development. Over the next five years or so, products will emerge from vendors' laboratories. In addition to evolution of current products, however, it is important to consider bolder developments that might take place. Chapter 5 explores such wild-card options.

CHAPTER 5

Softer Software:
The Groupware Wild Card

ROBERT JOHANSEN AND PAUL SAFFO

Softer software[1] is software that is at once easier to use and more powerful than applications available today. Much progress has been made toward softer software through advances in interface design, but further advances must come from other quarters. The key technology developments for softer software are being fueled by the commercialization of advanced programming, particularly AI techniques, concepts, and technologies. Indeed, we feel that AI will be the single most important technical contributor to groupware growth. Much of this contribution will not be pure AI, however, nor will it necessarily be perceived by groupware users as AI. Rather, we expect AI spin-off technologies—often operating behind the scenes—to be most important.

AI is a field of computer science that is just beginning to realize solid and successful commercial applications. (It is a field that has been trying for over two decades to become an overnight success.) For many—AI professionals and users alike—the discipline's failure to live up to the promises of early AI evangelists has been cause for criticism. This pattern, however, obscures that fact that AI as a field has achieved limited but important gains in the course of failing to realize larger objectives. These limited gains often are of only secondary interest to AI researchers in search of bigger game, and they are overlooked by critics who emphasize the relative lack of commercial success.

This chapter is built on the observation that this underapplied body of understandings—AI techniques, technologies, and concepts—represents an important opportunity for groupware product providers and users. The results will not be perceived by users as AI, but simply as systems that are easier and more effective to use. Softer software is a key wild card that could greatly affect groupware

"THIS IS SOMETHING THE COMPUTER
PEOPLE WILL REALLY LOVE. IT'S HARDER
THAN SOFTWARE, AND SOFTER THAN HARDWARE."

growth. Softer software will mean faster groupware takeoff and more important applications.

The guiding question to ask is how the addition of AI technologies to groupware can more effectively satisfy user needs, and in turn, how do new product opportunity areas affect projected needs? We believe product planning is most effective when it is also incremental, a systematic process of identifying opportunities and responding to user experiences. We consciously avoid recommendations involving heavy technological pushes or great leaps of marketing faith.

AI DEFINED

At its broadest, AI "is the part of computer science concerned with designing intelligent computer systems, that is, systems that exhibit the characteristics we associate with intelligence in human behavior—understanding language, learning, reasoning, solving problems, and so on," a definition articulated by Stanford computer scientist Edward Feigenbaum in 1981.[2] Underlying this definition is the notion that human thought ultimately is a logical process capable of being represented formally. Although this definition might be of interest to philosophers and clerics—it ultimately forces one to ask what human intelligence is—it offers little more to the task at hand than the reassurance that AI is a large enough field to conceal many hidden nuggets that may be useful in groupware products.

A less-reverent approach to AI is captured in the oft-quoted cynic's definition of AI: "For academics, AI is *a*nything *i*mpossible. For marketeers, it is *a*nything *i*nteresting. For the military, it is *a*nything *i*nvincible. And, finally, for users, AI is *a*nything *i*mproved."

Perhaps the most useful definition is that credited to MIT researcher Patrick Winston, who observed that AI is concerned with getting computers to do things that would make human beings look smart. This is a pragmatic statement that encompasses AI advances without becoming snarled in philosophical issues. Unless explicitly stated otherwise, this is the primary definition used in this chapter. A variation of Winston's definition can be used to stimulate groupware ideas: AI is concerned with using computers to do tasks that previously only human beings could do, but if done by machines, would free human beings to do more important things.

The goals set by AI researchers are both diverse and ambitious, but generally they encompass the creation of highly capable systems by modeling processes that—when performed by people—would be called intelligence or reasoning.

AI has, for the last two decades, *seemed* tantalizingly close to achieving major breakthroughs. Despite ongoing research efforts, and over five years of intense commercial activity, the field of AI has yet to realize its ambitious goals. Promises made by researchers in the 1960s and 1970s are still being made today. Breakthroughs are still being touted as "just around the corner," but they are likely to remain out of reach for at least the near future.

Against a backdrop of marketing hype and frustrated expectations, it is easy to overlook the fact that AI has made considerable progress, contributing in important ways to computer science generally and providing products for a small but growing commercial industry. This progress is often hidden because from the perspective of AI professionals, compared to yet unmet research goals, it seems trivial. Many of AI's most prominent researchers seem to define AI as "anything we *cannot* do with computers," with the result that anything actually achieved is cast out of the field. In the early 1960s, for example, spelling checkers were considered AI, as were programs capable of playing chess. Today, commercial applications of both are commonplace, though these applications are no longer considered AI—and, in fact, are largely implemented without use of current AI technologies. In the rush to meet ambitious goals, small wins (from a technological point of view) have been ignored and underexploited.

It is precisely the undramatic, overlooked understandings—similar to those that led to products such as spelling checkers—that we are expecting in the groupware field. Our research process has been one of revisiting these understandings and examining them from a groupware perspective. The process is not unlike sifting through a heap of crumpled notes for overlooked ideas discarded by AI researchers. Time and again, we have encountered interesting applications of these discarded understandings, typically described something like: "This really isn't AI, but it works and is kind of interesting." For our part, it is not only interesting; the "discards" may satisfy a variety of groupware needs, from scheduling to user interface and from graphics preparation to network configuration.

KEY CONCEPTS FOR GROUPWARE

The AI field encompasses a broad range of disparate subdisciplines and concepts—from expert systems to robotics and computer vision. We have selected a core set of concepts that we think are most important in pursuing groupware opportunities. Several of these concepts would not normally be included in a narrow definition of AI. Each of these areas has the promise of offering understanding useful in the groupware area; in our opinion, however, some are of greater immediate interest than others. With this in mind, we have arranged the list in Table 9 to emphasize concepts of particular relevance to groupware.

Hypertext/hypermedia describes any computer-based system employing nonlinear structuring of information in text, graphic, or other forms (for example, audio or motion video) to allow associative indexing of specific parts of an information base. Hypermedia systems typically employ "links" between discrete pieces of data accessible by the user. Thus a user can either elect to read a single text

Table 9 KEYS TO SOFTER SOFTWARE

Very Relevant	Less Directly Relevant
Hypermedia: nonlinear, multipath structuring of information to allow flexible search, restructuring, and presentation of ideas; works like a thesaurus, building on links to allow associative indexing	Computer vision: conversion of images to computer-recognizable form
	Robotics: computer-based flexible manipulation and control
WYSIWIS: what *you* see *is* what *I* see; expresses the notion of a shared visual information space	Automated programming: machine-generated programming from high-level (especially natural) language
Agents: "intelligent" systems capable of acting on behalf of human beings	
Inheritance: a term for the notion that the properties of an item or object are acquired from the categories of which they are instances	
Expert systems: systems that represent and apply human expertise	
Natural language generation: machine production of natural language (for example, English) text	
Natural language understanding: computer understanding of human language from text in computer-readable form	
Knowledge media: concept emphasizing AI tools for linking people; not just for stand-alone systems	

in linear form or select and follow multiple links to other texts or graphics. The notion of hypermedia was first articulated by Ted Nelson in the mid-1960s as hypertext,[3] though the notion of associative indexing is much older—traceable at least to an article, "As We May Think," written by Vannevar Bush for the July 1945 issue of the *Atlantic Monthly*.[4] In any sense, the hypertext concept merely amounts to bringing to computers the same flexibility we already enjoy in print. A thesaurus is a paper version of hypertext. It has no single beginning or end. Each time a thesaurus is consulted, the reader enters at a different location based on the word he or she is trying to escape from. Then, the reader follows a unique path through its references determined by what is discovered along the way, finally exiting when a satisfactory word is found. The first commercial hypertext systems are just beginning to appear on the market.[5] Apple's Hypercard package has created an operating system environment for the Macintosh that allows others to develop hypertext applications.[6]

In a group setting such links could be among text, graphics, and digital audio or video. Applications of hypermedia include authoring systems for nonlinear writings, interactive training systems, and as index systems for large, multimedia databases. In addition, hypertext systems are already being sold as an alternative to idea processors. Finally, we have found the hypermedia notion to be a powerful concept for introducing business people to examples of how AI and groupware complement each other.

WYSIWIS stands for *what you see is what I see*. This term initially referred to situations in which participants in a meeting each saw precisely the same image on their computer screens. However, this strict definition is being relaxed to include less-precise match ups. WYSIWIS is a good shorthand for the notion of a shared electronic information space.

Such capabilities have an especially significant value in electronic meetings in which the exchange of visual information (charts, graphs, pictures) is required.[7]

Agents is a term popularized by computer pioneer Alan Kay (now a Fellow at Apple Computer) that refers to the concept of AI programs capable enough to operate on behalf of human users. Examples of agents include: programs that can search through databases for desired information, changing the definition of what is being sought "on the fly," based on the data found; programs autonomously and intelligently able to control telecommunications equipment; and programs that learn the preferences and habits of human users to make system interfaces more responsive. A key criterion of a fully implemented agent is autonomy; that is, how willing a human being is to relinquish control to the agent. No examples of true agents exist today, but more-limited implementations abound: "mailer demons" (programs that automatically notify senders of electronic messages that could not be delivered to an intended recipient on another system) on many time-sharing systems are but one example. Several researchers have created "news agents"—programs that search through major news databases (such as AP, UPI, or Dow Jones) and assemble custom "newspapers" tailored to their creators' preferences. The creation of highly autonomous agents is a major goal of current U.S. Department of Defense (DOD) initiatives, so it is possible that significant advances will occur in this area over the next five years.

Applications of agents in groupware might include bandwidth agents capable of dynamically reassigning specific bandwidth on demand according to group needs, agents capable of identifying and "signing up" participants in conferences on particular topics, reminder agents that help human participants to remember commitments, and topic agents that monitor a broad range of on-line conferences and alert their human sponsor when items of interest arise. Agents could, of course, be used in more-intrusive applications, such as identifying people who express unpopular opinions.

Inheritance is a label for the notion that the properties of a particular object—a piece of text, a graphic, or an icon—are derived from its relationship to the category to which it belongs. For example, a cat inherits the properties of the animal category, of which it is a member. In a computing environment, an object classified under a certain category would automatically be given—inherit—the characteristics of that category. The term *inheritance* is derived from object-oriented programming, a branch of computer science closely related to AI. The origins of the term can be traced to Simula, a precursor of modern, object-oriented programming languages, originally designed to facilitate the writing of simulation programs.

Groupware applications of inheritance are subtle, but important. For example, inheritance concepts could be incorporated into computer conferencing: a user could build a custom conference structure by assembling individual components (for example, messaging with automatic reminder functions or distribution functions) into a new file. Similar applications in the graphics area might permit users to build custom icon-based command structures by combining individual command symbols.

Expert systems (also called *knowledge-based systems,* because they encode human knowledge) is an area of AI that has enjoyed the greatest commercial success to date. Our assessment is that under 100 end-user expert systems (systems containing specific expert knowledge for specific applications) are presently being offered for sale, and only a small number of companies are using internally developed systems. The essence of expert system applications is the embedding of human expert knowledge into a computer system for application by human beings to specific problems through a limited natural-language interface. Because the cost of designing such systems is relatively high, vendors of expert systems such as Teknowledge (Palo Alto, California) and Intellicorp (Mountain View, California) have emphasized their use to overcome human bottlenecks—situations in which a company's growth is limited by a few human experts who require years of experience before they become fully productive. Classic examples of such applications include drilling and exploration advisor programs for use in oil companies, system-configuration advisors for computer manufacturers, and medical advisors for use in evaluating specialized disorders. The cost of expert-system shells—special AI packages that greatly simplify the process of creating an expert system—has dropped dramatically and promises to drop further in the near future.

Such systems could be especially useful in making complex tasks tractable and making complex communications procedures simple. Expert systems hold particular promise for rapid application into groupware products, particularly for making "softer systems"—using dollops of expertise to simplify use and operation. Examples of such applications are an expert system for designing intelligible overhead projection slides, taking into account audience and room size and specific projection equipment to be used, as well as general graphic design principles; a line volume/noise analyzer that analyzes and automatically cleans up line noise; least-cost routing advisors; and facility-scheduling advisors.

Natural language generation (and speech generation) is concerned with developing systems that can communicate accurately with people by producing "natural language" (for example, English) text. Limited natural language capabilities have been effectively implemented. When combined with advances in speech generation—the conversion of machine-readable text into synthetically generated speech output—even limited natural-language-generation systems can have effective product applications. These systems can be implemented on even low-end personal computers without special voice synthesis chips, though such chips are finding application in everything from advanced fighter jets to low-cost consumer electronics.

This technology is already finding applications in telecommunications products, including voice "time stamps" on an answering machine's message recordings, voice prompts on voice-mail systems, and on audiotex systems (one such system is used to dispatch airline personnel). In addition, if used in conjunction with expert systems, natural language generation could be used in groupware tasks such as teletraining (for mock-up and role-playing exercises), as well as more-applied tasks, including group process support and as a participant greeter on audio bridges.

Natural language understanding (and speech recognition) is concerned with developing systems that can understand human language presented in machine-readable form. Such systems could be used as components of human translation systems for electronic meetings. Limited natural language capabilities have been effectively implemented, with approximately 10 companies already active in the area. These systems can understand isolated queries and statements within limited, predefined domains. More-comprehensive systems capable of understanding all queries regardless of context remain a partially fulfilled goal.

Speech recognition involves the conversion of the spoken word into machine-readable form. Speech recognition is the front end of natural language understanding systems: recognition precedes understanding. Limited speech recognition—limited-vocabulary, speaker-dependent systems—is already a commercial reality. Approximately 25 companies are active sellers of such systems. Users of speech recognition products include United Parcel, Max Factor, and Blue Cross. However, comprehensive speech recognition systems capable of managing context-independent, and/or speaker-independent communications will not be realized soon. Several entities, particularly the DOD, have major initiatives under way in this area, and thus surprises may lie ahead. Research on more-advanced systems will become ever more closely tied to research in natural language understanding. In the meantime, we will see systems grouped into two categories: those capable of recognizing a limited vocabulary spoken by any of a large population of speakers and those capable of recognizing a larger vocabulary uttered by a small group, often only a single individual.

Systems including limited natural language understanding and speech recognition have important capabilities for groupware. Examples include voice-activated dialers (available in telephones costing under $300), voice-prompted system features, voice recognition log-on access for conferencing systems, voice-based scheduling, and voice recognition of conference call participants as an input into an intelligent meeting "secretary" or text display identifying the current speaker for other participants.

Knowledge media is a concept articulated by computer scientist Mark Stefik at Xerox's PARC.[8] Instead of building only autonomous programs, a perhaps larger and complementary goal is to build interactive knowledge media—information networks encompassing semiautomated services for the generation, distribution, and consumption of knowledge. Viewed differently, a knowledge media approach argues in favor of making the entire communications system an intelligent agentlike device. This is a minority view of the AI world, but Mark Stefik is very well regarded, and we expect the notion of knowledge media to become a starting point for many future efforts.

The implications of knowledge media for groupware are enormous. Instead of designing robust systems capable of dealing with complex and uncertain external communications environments, we should be building intelligent communications environments. Although standards would help, the knowledge media approach does not depend on standards. From an interface perspective, a knowledge media approach might imply that one should not talk into a telephone or look at a screen, but instead "step inside" the telephone or the screen—have the media surround the user in a special room—and have the media supported by intelligent systems. Electronic meetings conducted in a knowledge media environment would be especially useful for sustaining group participation when the communication is nonsimultaneous; the history and direction of the conference could be sustained with closely intertwined documentation and maps.

Computer vision, the ability of computers to recognize shapes and forms, is a relatively mature but limited commercial market—limited at the moment to industrial applications. Current vision systems are computationally intensive and require relatively constrained environments—carefully controlled lighting and a limited universe of possible three-dimensional objects—to function effectively. As of 1987, over 100 companies offered vision products. Major research efforts funded by the DOD and major corporate sponsors make it possible that more-robust systems capable of operating in varied environments and with unknown objects will become a reality in the time frame contemplated in this book.

Vision processing is a subarea of computer vision much closer to general commercial realization because, unlike industrial computer vision, vision processing does not automatically require real-time processing. This overcomes the need to have high-powered computers available for processing activities. Much vision-processing work has already been done in connection with interpretation of aerial photos and remote sensing data.

Absent from dramatic advances in computational power (such as a commercial introduction of neural network computing) and computer vision technology, it is hard to imagine affordable applications realistically achievable as groupware products within the foreseeable future. The prospect for vision processing applications in group communication is brighter, however. Such applications could include systems capable of converting graphic images into data or systems capable of interpreting graphics to determine whether their resolution is sufficient for transmission on specific communications systems.

Robotics is defined here to refer primarily to intelligent manipulation and control. The term is derived from the Czech *Robota,* meaning slavery, and was first used by the playwright Karel Capek in the 1931 play *R.U.R.* to refer to an autonomous mechanical simulation. Robotics is an area that has already enjoyed considerable commercial application in areas of relatively limited flexibility of application. We have limited function industrial robots, but the creation of a robot in the sense contemplated by Capek probably will not occur in the near future.

A robot-oriented approach to equipment command and control—in effect, turning communications equipment into stationary robots—could have interesting applications for electronic meetings. Applications include a robot cameraman—a stationary video robot capable of tracking participants as they move around a room.

Programmer activity is becoming a major crisis for the computer industry; *automated programming*—intelligent creation of software code from human requests—may be a long-term solution. In many respects, automated software development is a close cousin to natural language programming, except that the former has the advantage of working within a more closely defined and constrained environment. Nonetheless, the creation of automated programming systems is proving more difficult than anticipated. Commercial systems offering automated programming capabilities exist today, but they often force significant performance trade-offs compared to code written by human beings. Still, given the high and increasing cost of programmers and the falling cost of high-performance processors, it is a trade-off that often proves favorable. It is quite possible that we will see major breakthroughs in this area within the next few years.

Strategies developed in this area may have applications for automation of routine communications tasks. At the same time, this area is in competition with advances in high-level languages for user attention. Applications in groupware include systems capable of tailoring (customizing) complex interfaces to match the preferences of specific users and the use of automated programming techniques for low-cost routing and logical connection of telecommunications links.

It is difficult to array these concepts in a structure that formally expresses the interrelationships between them, because the interrelationships are much more complex than any such structure tends to suggest. Rather than mapping the crisp features on, say, a prairie, the process is more like identifying shifting channels in a swamp. Table 10 reflects our judgment, based on the relative maturity and availability of each concept, regarding the interrelationships. Note that, depending on how broadly one defines each, any single concept could be placed in several locations on the map, or even cover the map entirely.

Because AI remains in a highly developmental stage, we expect the field will undergo important changes and advances within the next five years. Several of these changes will have particular significance for the link to groupware:

AI as a separate area of commercial application may be less important than AI spin-off applications. In short, most of AI may be absorbed into numerous application areas. As noted, AI has taken over 20 years to begin delivering some commercial successes. One reason may be that AI techniques—especially expert

Table 10   AVAILABILITY AND MATURITY OF AI CONCEPTS

Mature			
Natural language generation			
Expert systems			
Robotics			
WYSIWIS	Agents		
Speech recognition	Automated programming	Natural language understanding	
Hypertext	Vision		
	Knowledge Media	Hypermedia	
Immature			

Today			Future

When Available?

systems, the first application of AI to find commercial success—are so tied to other non-AI applications areas that ultimately AI technologies may cease to exist as independent products. Users will not buy AI; they will buy business applications that incorporate AI techniques and concepts. As such, the incorporation of AI understandings into another application area may become a dominant commercial model for the field.

AI's most comprehensive, well-publicized goals will remain tantalizingly out of reach, but much progress will be made on less-ambitious goals. The basic objectives of AI—the creation of intelligent, autonomous systems—are so inextricably linked to an understanding of the processes of human thought that the realization of those objectives may not occur within any commercially reasonable time frame. Many of the most fundamental goals of AI seem more out of reach now than they did in the mid-1960s. The more experts come to understand these problems, the more intractable they seem to become. Less-ambitious goals will be realized, and commercial use of AI will continue to increase, however.

The notion of knowledge media is emerging as a significant new perspective on AI. This trend represents an extension of the previous two trends, for it is both an example of new ways of thinking about AI and a case in which AI is most meaningful when tied to applications—in this case, human-machine communications.

More AI technology—particularly expert systems—will become available in the form of silicon. More and more AI tools, including inference engines (the software that operates on expert-system knowledge bases) and expert-system shells will be imbedded into chips. This will make such systems very much faster than systems today—in certain cases very much cheaper. The net effect will be the availabiltiy and practicality of including such chip-based systems in teleconferencing hardware (including even basic telephones) without excessive cost and with no loss of performance.

The cost of AI building-block technologies will continue to drop dramatically. The cost of basic building-block systems—AI language, especially expert system shells—has already dropped dramatically. In late 1983 the typical expert system shell cost close to $100,000 and required a host minicomputer. In 1984 the cost dropped to approximately $50,000, and by 1985 slightly more limited systems were being offered for use on PCs at a cost of just over $10,000. In 1987, costs are well below $1,000 for many shells, and some are less than $100. Because the cost of the shells proper has little room to drop further, the main cost changes will be for *run-time kernels* (the essential software engine required to support a finished system) incorporated in completed systems. AI languages have followed similar curves, so that today it is possible to purchase a full implementation of Lisp and Prolog (the two leading AI languages) for under $500. Finished products—expert systems containing expert knowledge—may not enjoy the same price drop, because the value of the encoded expertise will ultimately determine the price of such systems.

PC-based systems will prove a key growth area. Combined with the lowered cost of expert system tools, this will be critical for rapid advances in AI. The lowered cost and greatly increased capabilities of PCs will allow individual programmers to develop AI systems. This trend will greatly diffuse technical understandings of AI; what was once the complex and arcane preserve of a few Ph.D.s will become accessible to curious hobbyists and serious amateurs, as well as to people seeking to add a taste of AI to other products under development.

SOME GROUPWARE IDEAS

We have developed a set of groupware-related product concepts or features that could grow from softer software. These areas are listed in Table 11.

Process advisors involve application of AI technology or techniques to group process tasks. Examples of process advisor products might include group or organizational protocol guides, commitment coordinators, conflict managers, group process coaches, and group brainstorming aids. For example, a research system called Cognoter at Xerox PARC[9] guides a group through the various stages of brainstorming and supports this idea-development process. As already mentioned, expert systems have enjoyed greater commercial success than has any other area of AI, and so there is a rich lode of AI technology to draw on for ideas. Process advisors can have more or less understanding of the subject matter a group is discussing. The more content the advisor has to understand, the more difficult (and more expensive) it will be to implement.

Interaction trackers are systems that help human participants identify patterns in group communications having significance for the communication itself. Such products do not require AI technology to be implemented. For example, a participation rate tracker on a computer conferencing system could simply keep a tally of who sent which messages to whom about a particular subject, and how often. This information could be useful in determining whether the interests of particular members were being adequately represented in a group decision-making process. Addition of AI technology, implementing, say, an expert system–based participation tickler that prods underparticipating members to speak up could add considerable value to the product. Other products falling within the interaction tracker category might include intelligent comment chainers (for example, a system that chained comments of various

Table 11   PRODUCT CONCEPT CATEGORIES
Process advisors
Interaction trackers
Translators
Intelligent tutors
Intelligent interfaces
Adaptive networks

participants in different ways—chronologically, by subject, or by opinion) and goal-achievement aids (for example, task ticklers or motivational advisors). One could also imagine issues-tracking programs that, for example, search interoffice communications and alert managers to emerging organizational or workload problems.

Translators offer both natural (for example, English) language translation and computer language translation (for example, between different languages or protocols). This category quickly runs up against the limits of current AI technology. For example, even limited natural language translation from computer-readable text is still not a commercial reality. Ideally, groupware users could benefit greatly from a simultaneous voice translator for international calls. But more-limited products could be more immediately implemented. For example, telephones that recognize limited voice commands are already on the market. This same technology applied to carefully constrained group communications environments could be dramatically useful; an example might be a voice-controlled video display for use during a computer-supported meeting.

On the machine translation end, protocol transfers could be used to make otherwise incompatible hardware work together. A *black box* containing an expert system capable of making a best guess about what hardware is on the other end of a line could act as a "systems diplomat" working for detente among various pieces of communications hardware. A third product possibility in this area might be products capable of interpreting graphic information as text or numbers.

Intelligent tutors reflect the application of expert system technology to human learning. In the groupware area, it could be used to assist people learning to use unfamiliar communications products. Such tutors could be limited to use of a specific system—a practical solution for overcoming the problems of learning (or relearning) infrequently used systems. More-ambitious applications might include some sort of general reasoning advisor.

Intelligent interfaces take the learning process a step farther than intelligent tutors. Rather than helping a person to learn how to use a complex system, an intelligent-interface approach would place the AI technology into the system directly, putting more of the learning burden on the system itself. The most obvious applications are at the man-machine interface; the next step beyond current user-friendly interfaces will be intelligent interfaces that are not only friendly but capable of adapting to the user's idiosyncrasies as well. Other product opportunities lie in creating machine-friendly interfaces. This is the opposite of the translator "system diplomat" mentioned earlier; instead of the external system's working harder to understand the local system, the local system would reconfigure itself to work with the outsider, not unlike an American business person learning several foreign languages, rather than expecting foreigners to speak English.

Adaptive networks refer to the use of AI to create electronic networks capable of shifting connections in response to changing use patterns. This is a category that already is exhibiting significant commercial activity. The systems already in existence draw heavily on expert-systems technology and typically act as advisors to human operators rather than acting autonomously. For example, one current product assists operators in prioritizing and filtering network monitor alarms.

CONCLUSION

Softer software could make groupware much more attractive and much more useful. AI spin-offs are key to this growth path. Although much of the AI world is focusing on big wins, there is a window of opportunity for companies that understand how to apply AI spin-off technology, techniques, and concepts on a smaller scale. We have concluded that small wins (from an AI perspective) can have major impacts on groupware. Furthermore, some of the these small wins are immediately available, as an increasing number of companies are beginning to prove.

AI is not a field that is easy to understand, however, either for vendors or for users. It is a field that has already been oversold by the popular business press. Business-user backlashes are occurring as it becomes clear that the promises of AI are coming more slowly than advertised.

In our analysis, we have identified a few concepts that we think are important to understanding the groupware opportunities presented by AI and other forms of softer software. It is important to note that one concept we judge to be very useful in thinking about communications of AI—hypermedia—is usually not thought of as an AI concept at all. This is one indication of a general conclusion we have reached: the current field of AI does not match up directly with business opportunities in the groupware marketplace. There is a need for bridge building and idea generation. On one hand, this is disappointing, because considerable prework must be done to translate AI experiences into business opportunities in groupware. On the other hand, complete clarity of options would mean that the market would have already happened. There are still real opportunities for major innovations in this field.

CHAPTER 6

The Outlook for Groupware

ROBERT JOHANSEN

Groupware will become a major user application area, but probably neither quickly nor simply. Before evaluating the specifics of growth in the market for groupware, it is important to consider the overall environment within which groupware will emerge. As we discussed in Chapter 3, various levels of infrastructure are needed to support groupware products. In thinking about how such an infrastructure might develop, we see a variety of possible scenarios. In this chapter, looking out 5 to 10 years, we present nine that explore alternatives. These scenarios are all believable, and they express the underlying uncertainty of the groupware market. For each scenario we discuss (1) the scenario in summary, (2) the primary product concepts, (3) likely vendor types, (4) user issues, (5) technology, (6) the competitive climate, and (7) uncertainties.

These scenarios paint a complex picture—concepts, players, events—that could occur as groupware products and services are introduced. The purpose here is not to predict the future, but to understand the dynamics of new technologies at work and the range of possible outcomes. Such complexity means that even though the pace of groupware activity is increasing, large-scale products will come on the market slowly. The next two to five years will be a period of early exploration and positioning.

The nine scenarios have been descriptively titled:

Computer at the Core
Personal Solutions
Dominant Duopoly
Network at the Core
All Together Now
Ten Years After
Magic Box

PBX at the Core
Face-to-Face First

The relationships among scenarios and the question of ordering are discussed after the scenarios are presented.

SCENARIO 1: COMPUTER AT THE CORE

A computer manufacturer offers a PBX as a peripheral device for the computer rather than having the computer as an auxiliary PBX processor. If the proper marketing connections can be made, the prospect of a computer at the core is attractive for computer manufacturers. Everyone who has a telephone needs computer hardware. In addition, this scenario probably offers the smoothest transition for the customer in moving from using the terminal device as pure telephone to using it as a computer terminal, to using it as a groupware terminal.

PRIMARY PRODUCT CONCEPTS: Groupware is viewed primarily as a series of features available within computing environments. Multimedia capabilities are available, all switched through the central system. Some telephony functions could be handled in a similar (and integrated) fashion. Early adopters will be distributed engineering work groups with links to manufacturing and marketing groups.

LIKELY VENDORS: Current vendors of computer mainframes and perhaps minicomputers, or even micros.

USER ISSUES: Can group-oriented communications be delivered via mainframes, both from a technical point of view and in terms of service support? Communications functions certainly vary from those of data processing; can they coexist in the same computer? Is it worth investing in a facility with groupware capabilities that may not be used immediately?

TECHNOLOGY: Computers continue to become more powerful and faster, making it easier to consider using them for additional functions. Voice-recognition capabilities could speed acceptance.

COMPETITIVE CLIMATE: IBM has held an enviable dominance over the mainframe market for many years. Given the parameters of this scenario, it would be hard to budge the giant.

UNCERTAINTIES: Although mainframes still dominate the computer market in terms of sales, they are perceived as workhorses rather than as products destined to lead us to new heights in communications and computing. The telecommunications market is not the mainframe market. Can mainframe manufacturers learn to be credible PBX suppliers? Will customers—who are used to sticking their PBXs in unused broom closets—be willing to accept the additional service requirements of yet another real computer on the premises?

SCENARIO 2: PERSONAL SOLUTIONS

The small software companies that began offering screen-sharing software in the mid-1980s have built the basis for a very large market. Other software options emerge for groupware, using a variety of media. In short, groupware becomes just another form of PC software.

PRIMARY PRODUCT CONCEPTS: Software that focuses on specific aspects of the communications process (for example, screen sharing of PC outputs, messaging, conferencing, shared writing space). The products are offered as components, but overall success of the market depends on interconnection of the various components.

LIKELY VENDORS: The software companies (Ashton-Tate, Microsoft, Lotus, and so on) have the inside track under this scenario. Very small companies are leading the early explorations, however, and it is possible that one of them could gain an edge. Beyond software companies, modem manufacturers are another likely player, as are the computer manufacturers themselves.

USER ISSUES: Packaging of many software products into one integrated environment is likely to be difficult. Quality control and interconnection are also issues, particularly as many small players are involved. Users will look for integrated systems.

TECHNOLOGY: Software development is the main event here, working within specific computing environments that are pretty much already here. AI techniques and concepts are likely to play a major role in the evolution of this software. Interconnection standards will also be very important.

COMPETITIVE CLIMATE: Cut-throat competition among the software companies is likely during the early stages, at least until the market leaders emerge. Joint ventures and strategic relationships will be highly sought after.

UNCERTAINTIES: Can a groupware market be built up from software? Can the components be made to fit together adequately? Will necessary standards be adopted and implemented?

SCENARIO 3: DOMINANT DUOPOLY

Two major players (or at most a small number) emerge to dominate the market for groupware. Such players build on on existing network infrastructure, probably their own.

PRIMARY PRODUCT CONCEPTS: Both network-based and PC-based products are available, with standards set by the dominant providers. The products will almost certainly be limited if this scenario occurs, but they will also tend to be more dependable. Cautious expansion will be the theme.

LIKELY VENDORS: IBM, AT&T, and the regional Bell companies are most likely to be the dominant players under this scenario. Other vendors will concentrate on niches and accept the standards set by the duopoly.

USER ISSUES: Users have dependable options available, but within clear limits (that is, those specified by the dominant providers) and at a substantial price. Rather than optimizing either functionality or price, emphasis is on standardization and dependability. It is difficult to get special treatment in this sellers' market.

TECHNOLOGY: There are major R&D efforts by the major providers, but the pace of technology development is established by these companies rather than market forces. In general, technology is somewhat slower at being developed than under competitive scenarios. Interconnection technology should do very well.

COMPETITIVE CLIMATE: Smaller companies or new entrants have a very tough time under this scenario. The dominant players create barriers to entry wherever possible and users are reluctant to buy from "nonstandard" providers.

UNCERTAINTIES: Regulatory issues could easily arise under such a scenario, because competition would be definitely restrained by the factors mentioned previously. This scenario could also bring back some bad memories from large users, who would be inclined to develop new ways to bypass the dominant duopoly. If the duopoly becomes too complacent, opportunities for entry from the sidelines would emerge.

SCENARIO 4: NETWORK AT THE CORE

The telephone network becomes the primary home for groupware. It builds on the network conference calling, offering a wide range of new services using a variety of media. Compatibility problems are solved (to the extent they are solvable) at the network level. The user now has the opportunity to install communication processors between user terminals or keysets and outside network facilities. The most common example is likely to be a gateway between an LAN and an external analog or digital network. The user will be unaware of the distinction between processing in a box belonging to the user organization and processing in a box belonging to the telephone company. Variants of this scenario could build on LANs or other private networks.

PRIMARY PRODUCT CONCEPTS: Bridging and interconnection for a wide variety of products and media. Electronic messaging services are likely to be very important building blocks for more advanced services. Both use-sensitive and bulk rates are offered.

LIKELY VENDORS: AT&T and the regional Bell companies, obviously. Other carriers could be involved, as could providers of private networks. Manufacturers of PCs and other terminal devices may also be major players in the market, adapting their products to network protocols.

USER ISSUES: The bypass mentality has left many users uncomfortable with any dependence on central network services. Many users now operate their own networks, with interconnections to public networks as needed. Large users tend to be nervous under this scenario.

TECHNOLOGY: The network becomes the environment within which technology will develop. Even with the continuing trend toward miniaturization and simplification, there are some facilities that are most effective when their cost is shared by large numbers of users. The network provides a natural channel for providing and amortizing such facilities.

COMPETITIVE CLIMATE: Heavy competition among carriers around both price and service. Clearly, AT&T and the regional Bell companies would have the inside track. This could be a one-winner scenario, although such a network would certainly create opportunities for others to deliver services over the network.

UNCERTAINTIES: What are the limits of the network regarding types of information that can be exchanged? Can the carriers maintain these types of services? Will the message standardization efforts actually prove workable on a large scale? What are the problems of capitalizing the network capacity that will be required? Who will develop the advanced facilities to be offered?

SCENARIO 5: ALL TOGETHER NOW

The small- and medium-sized providers offer enough interconnection and compatibility so that a "chain" of services is possible without reliance on a small number of large providers.

PRIMARY PRODUCT CONCEPTS: Many product concepts emerge under this scenario, with a very wide range of options.

LIKELY VENDORS: Almost anyone.

USER ISSUES: Keeping up with the marketplace is difficult, because the schedules for introduction are erratic and fast paced. "Sole sourcing" is very difficult. Few preferred distribution channels emerge. Users may favor industry regulation.

TECHNOLOGY: This is a "let a thousand flowers bloom" philosophy, with many developments but very little in technology advancement. Thus, overall technology growth will be uncoordinated—even though much activity will be visible.

COMPETITIVE CLIMATE: Highly competitive, but with a sensitivity toward the dependence each provider has on other providers who are "above" or "below" on the service chain. Joint ventures and turnkey efforts are very popular. Franchising may occur.

UNCERTAINTIES: This scenario could not evolve without an underlying set of standards. The anarchy of the PC software market has been balanced by the predominance of the IBM PC, for example. What balancing factors could appear in the groupware realm?

SCENARIO 6: TEN YEARS AFTER

The promise of groupware is simply very slow in coming. A few innovative companies have successes, but the necessary pieces don't come together quickly. The next ten years are characterized by false starts, small wins, and unmet promises.

PRIMARY PRODUCT CONCEPTS: No coherent product themes emerge. Products exist in isolation, rather than in concert. Occasional creative efforts occur, but have little impact.

LIKELY VENDORS: No significant vendors make large-scale commitments. Several companies test the market, but nobody pushes into it.

USER ISSUES: Users are frustrated by a lack of unity in products. They find the groupware market too complicated to pursue in any big way. A few users develop their own internal systems, but they are companies with very sophisticated internal capabilities.

TECHNOLOGY: No major developments occur. Technology efforts do not contribute significantly to communications capabilities.

COMPETITIVE CLIMATE: Dull and unaggressive. Some start-ups fail. Software houses grow at a sluggish rate.

UNCERTAINTIES: Everyone believes that communications through computers will occur, but the issue is when? The longer it takes, the more skeptics there are.

Scenario 7: The Magic Box

Someone develops a *magic box* that integrates the telephone and the PC *at a reasonable price.* This box comes to be viewed as the new telephone (the equivalent of the horseless carriage), although it contains very powerful computing capabilities as well. The magic box becomes the connection point for groupware.

PRIMARY PRODUCT CONCEPTS: Beginning from basic telephony, this box gradually draws inexperienced users into functions that involve computing as well. Electronic messaging services and video displays with graphics are likely to be very important as a way of bringing in new users. Many other more-advanced systems will also emerge, building on this core concept.

LIKELY VENDORS: Major computer and communications companies all have a shot at developing such a box, as do some

PBX manufacturers. This may be a scenario in which one provider or architecture is dominant.

USER ISSUES: Picking the winner from the field of early entrants will be difficult. Controlling growth may actually be a problem.

TECHNOLOGY: This is where the "magic" must occur. The real sophistication will come with a union of technical capabilities and simplicity of use. Interconnection technology will be critical, because anything that replaces the telephone must obviously be universal. Add-on boards that offer new capabilities (for example, high-resolution graphics) will provide important building blocks, both for the magic box itself and for adapting conventional personal computers to allow communication with the magic box. In addition, AI concepts and techniques will be very important to make the box more useful and usable. *And,* all this must be done cheaply.

COMPETITIVE CLIMATE: Such a powerful building block will bring forth many new competitors. Although one very large provider may start the process, many smaller companies can benefit from the magic box because it has the potential of expanding the market so greatly.

UNCERTAINTIES: Can the magic be accomplished at the right price? Will users accept it and (if so) at what rate?

SCENARIO 8: PBX AT THE CORE

PBXs become the acknowledged home for groupware. Multimedia capabilities are available through PBXs and the marketplace assumes that this is the normal mode of operation.

PRIMARY PRODUCT CONCEPTS: Groupware is viewed primarily as a series of features offered over a PBX. All PBXs offer groupware functionality of some kinds, although it varies. The augmented capabilities of the PBX require keysets with enhanced displays. One of the main reasons that many of the current PBX capabilities remain largely unused is the terminal device. The common keyset, with its 12 buttons and lack of display, is insufficient to allow user control of many PBX functions.

LIKELY VENDORS: All major PBX and keyset providers. Other manufacturers provide groupware products or teleconferencing services or supplies to these providers. Under this scenario, only a few parts of the groupware marketplace survive outside of the PBX world.

USER ISSUES: Many of the vendor selection issues are simplified under this scenario, or at least centralized. The decision-making process for selecting PBXs could broaden, because more groups have a stake in the outcome. PBX systems have been centrally located and controlled. Operators typically have had limited skills. In this scenario, operators need to take a more active role in communications service delivery and management. A key issue: if the PBX is to be the primary home for groupware, the PBX must be able to compete with the microcomputer in the minds (and hearts) of users.

TECHNOLOGY: By definition, technology development in this scenario has to emerge within the realm of (or in connection with) PBXs. Given the increasingly open architectures, however, this is not much of a limitation. In a real sense, the way is cleared for aggressive new R&D efforts, because the general issues regarding where groupware "fits" are settled.

COMPETITIVE CLIMATE: The PBX market is highly competitive, and groupware creates a new battleground. Competitors without a PBX connection will be out of the game, or relegated to specific niches.

UNCERTAINTIES: What are the limits of PBXs to provide groupware functionalities? To what extent will the connection to the computing environment be gracefully implemented?

SCENARIO 9: FACE-TO-FACE FIRST

People need to understand groupware before they can consider buying it, and the most obvious way to teach them is to first use electronic aids for face-to-face meetings. When it becomes clear that computer aids can assist in meetings, people will realize that the same kind of communication can occur at a distance. This scenario assumes that firsthand experiences with in-room electronic support systems will lead to acceptance of groupware.

PRIMARY PRODUCT CONCEPTS: PCs can be used to provide electronic versions of paper flip charts. They can also provide a group memory through projection screens, with hard copy available for participants to take with them when the meeting is over. These same group support tools can be adapted for communication at a distance.

LIKELY VENDORS: Several small companies are already developing systems for electronic support of face-to-face meetings, but providers of visual aid equipment (for example, 3M or Eastman Kodak) are the most likely candidates.

USER ISSUES: Companies have never been anxious to spend money on equipment for conference rooms: most of today's rooms have only an overhead projector and perhaps a white board or flip charts. Also, conference rooms typically are not the responsibility of users in an organization. A few pioneers are adopting such meetings aids—internal users at Texas Instruments and Xerox, for example.

TECHNOLOGY: No radically new technology is needed to make this concept work, but adaptations will definitely be needed. Room display technologies are a particular problem, especially if costs are an issue.

COMPETITIVE CLIMATE: This scenario could catch companies sleeping, because it is an unusual angle. Competition would develop quickly as soon as the concept has caught on.

UNCERTAINTIES: Will users pay for electronic aids in conference rooms? Will they use the equipment if it is there? How quickly could this concept catch on? Will the connection between face-to-face meetings with electronic support and electronic meetings be an obvious step for users?

INTERPRETING THE SCENARIOS

The preceding scenarios were ordered in approximate likelihood of occurrence, but any such ranking is debatable. All these scenarios are believable, under the right conditions. The nine scenarios cluster into three groupings:

Institutional
Environmental
Entrepreneurial

Figure 18 summarizes the scenario clusters and suggests the patterns of dominance that we expect to see in the marketplace.

Institutional scenarios have the most strength, because they build on existing structures. People buy what they think they understand. If comfortable institutional structures already exist and communications through computers can be offered as a logical extension, they sell more easily. The three at-the-core scenarios (computer, network, and PBX) are the most logical institutional structures on which to build.

FIGURE 18
Groupware Infrastructure Scenarios

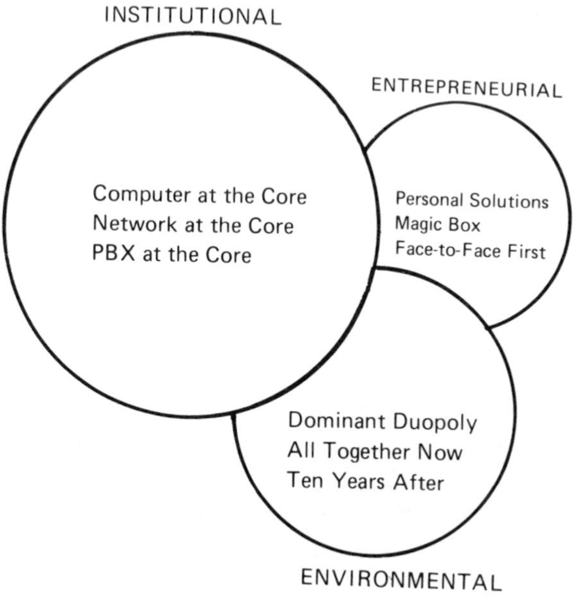

INSTITUTIONAL

ENTREPRENEURIAL

Computer at the Core
Network at the Core
PBX at the Core

Personal Solutions
Magic Box
Face-to-Face First

Dominant Duopoly
All Together Now
Ten Years After

ENVIRONMENTAL

Environmental scenarios are the next most powerful, in which the market environment dominates the emergence of groupware. Such forces, however, are very difficult to orchestrate for any purpose, including the introduction of new products and services. The Ten Years After scenario is the most overt expression of these problems, the one in which the market is simply very slow in developing. Such a scenario is certainly possible. The All Together Now scenario presents the flip side, in which all the providers orchestrate their own efforts. Only the Dominant Duopoly scenario presents a highly plausible path for the emergence of people communicating through computers. Some experts feel that this scenario is inevitable; it is just a question of how quickly it will occur.

Entrepreneurial angles on the marketplace face the most difficult obstacles, although at least two of the scenarios in this cluster are attractive. Indeed, Personal Solutions is already starting to happen, as software products for people communicating through computers are becoming increasingly common. The Magic Box could occur with the right product. Even a brilliant product is very difficult to develop in a purely grassroots fashion, however. The Magic Box scenario is much more likely to occur if it can be connected to institutional and/or environmental change processes.

The scenarios give alternate views of this future market. People who consider groupware products and services will be making assumptions, explicit or implicit, about how the infrastructure will develop. The nine scenarios in this chapter provide a good sense of the possibilities, but others could appear, or there could be combinations of the scenarios we have identified. The important thing for the reader at this point is to consider the nine scenarios, add others needed, and pick either one or a cluster that seems most likely or is most consistent with his or her goals.

PICK THE WINNERS

Figure 19 diagrams our understanding of how the markets for groupware will develop. The picture resembles a spearhead, with entrepreneurial efforts leading the way for environmental developments and, ultimately, institutional solutions. The time frame and the divisions between the parts of the figure are intentionally vague.

FIGURE 19

First-Breaking Groupware Efforts

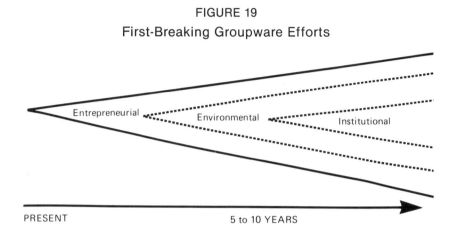

One can also think of the shape as an icebreaker that is opening up this new market just as an icebreaker opens a frozen sea.

Entrepreneurial efforts will spearhead the movement. They will use or create products quite selectively. These applications can include many people, but what makes them entrepreneurial is that they are in response to single problems or opportunities. They will begin as ad hoc solutions and successful applications, and spin-offs will be adopted permanently. Many of these attempts will fail and will never be heard of publicly. Over the next three to five years, though, many will succeed. By the end of five years, integrated applications will be much more common.

Enough of these applications in an organization or a market or a region will constitute an environment—a recognizable pattern of events. These changes could create a switch in a majority of businesses to voice messaging or the use of shared-screen computer-assisted design/computer-assisted manufacturing (CAD/CAM) by a large number of engineers. It implies that many profitable niches have been established in the three- to six-year time frame. Those environments that are robust, that have obvious payoffs, and that work well will be candidates to become institutional solutions.

The institutional structures will grow out of the most successful environments. They will be in areas that are accessible to the large players needed to act on that scale. As mentioned above, network-based services are the most likely candidate to be at the core of efforts to institutionalize communication through computers. In five years, some of the patterns of institutions will be apparent, though the roots will be in place well before that time.

OVERALL PROSPECTS

Looking beyond the infrastructure for groupware, it is possible to draw some general conclusions about prospects:

Existing technology is up to the job. Many promising technologies are still awaiting practical application. Most current groupware concepts can be executed using existing technology. Packaging is key.

The growth curve for groupware is likely to be discouraging to some vendors. There have been, and will continue to be, real discontinuities in the market. Progress will not occur gradually and constantly, despite the expectations, hopes, and projections of vendors. It is more likely that acceptance and market growth will come in fits and starts.

There is still an assimilation problem in the groupware market. The growth of this market is a partial function of the acceptance of the basic unit for many products: the PC. Many people are still becoming accustomed to the idea of having a PC on their desks or within easy access. Many have not yet become comfortable with the concept of using it for assistance in work tasks. And a very few have integrated the PC into their work activities as a regular tool. Until a large share of the potential user base has reached this level of comfort, a product based on the PC is unlikely to achieve mass acceptability.

The downside risks of groupware use are significant, but they are outweighed by the promises.

Each of the product categories discussed in Chapter 3 will have a life of its own, with some growth and many applications, some of which bear on groupware and most of which bear principally on some other function.

People will communicate through computers only when there is a real or perceived *need*. Needs (a term beaten beyond death) are occasions when communicating through computers is faster, less expensive, or more efficient than an alternative; computers must provide a unique channel, fill a recognized deficiency, or add significant value in some other way. The use of voice mail to eliminate rounds of telephone tag (though not to replace meetings or memos) is a perfect example of a need. Other applications will be in much narrower markets. Shared graphic screens, for example, will probably be a market confined to engineers and others in decentralized work groups.

An important side benefit of the spread of these technologies into such niches will be the exposure of users to the different capabilities of the systems. Voice mail users in an organization, for example, initially will applaud the gain in efficiency. The first person to discover and use the voice memo distribution function successfully will be regarded as a hotshot. If it saves him or her time or effort, other people will be sure to follow. At that point, a crucial threshold of awareness of the capabilities of computer-supported communication will have been passed. This awareness will not automatically transfer to other forms of computer communication, but each gain will contribute to a more receptive environment.

The result of this pattern of activity will be that no separate new industry called groupware is likely. There will be few unifying themes, no mass market, no technology or single institution at the core.

Nevertheless, there will be significant and profitable niches. Many of these will be occupied by small firms, many of them started expressly to exploit the niche. Large companies will find ways to participate, by focusing their efforts on a particular strength such as network services for AT&T or selling computers for IBM. The call is there, though, for joint ventures with smaller companies through specific applications. AT&T has led the way in this area, and other corporations are also becoming active.

In the longer term, it is network-based services offered by the regional Bell operating companies and the long distance carriers that have the best chance of pulling a coherent groupware market together. They have the technical muscle to wrestle some useful functions out of the network. It remains to be seen whether they can convince customers to use the services.

In the meantime, we expect that innovative user organizations will see the three- to five-year "delay" as a window of opportunity for them to gain competitive advantages through the use of computer-supported teams. In particular, we expect that user organizations with the following characteristics will be major users of groupware in the near future:

Companies with many decentralized project teams

Companies with a high penetration of personal computers and LANs

Companies with successful teleconferencing systems

Companies known for their flexible organizational structures

Companies with a track record for early adoption of innovations in information systems

The driving force over the next five years will be a collage of individual efforts, primarily from small providers and innovative users. We can expect several profitable niches to emerge and to expand gradually. In most cases, successful products and services will be (1) targeted toward specific user groups with strong incentives to use the new system, (2) extremely simple to install and use, and (3) showing a pattern of integration of existing technologies or small advances rather than state-of-the-art technologies.

In this five-year time frame, we expect that small software companies will lead the way. These will be high-risk ventures, however, because they will be leading the behavior-change efforts implied by group-oriented software. Small-service providers should be quite successful, because it will be feasible for them to package some of the benefits of computer-supported teams and to sell them as a service to users who do not want to undergo major development efforts themselves. The major manufacturers are not likely to take the lead; they will wait for the acceptance of groupware. The major software providers have real opportunities in the short run, but they are most likely to let the small companies do the R&D and test marketing for them. The successful small providers of group-oriented software will then become acquisition candidates. (Surprises could affect the speed of this development. Appendix B discusses several surprises that, if they occur, could have major impacts on the speed of groupware growth.)

In the longer term (5 to 10 years), we expect that groupware will "disappear" as a separate market and become a natural part of computer use, particularly PC use. The "banner" of groupware will no longer be needed, because products and user applications will be readily apparent to all concerned. Groupware will evolve from a new product class to a "feature" that is built into desktop computing.

In short, groupware will happen in a big way. The only questions are when and in what form—and who will make money from groupware growth. For the next three years, expect big wins by only a few players—innovative users, service providers, and small software companies. In the three- to five-year time frame, computer support for work teams will become much more accessible and much more heavily used. In the five- to ten-year time frame, groupware will become a fact of business life.

CHAPTER 7

Doing It Right

ROBERT JOHANSEN

Chapter 6 discussed the future of groupware, but Chapter 7 is aimed at people who want to create their own futures. Indeed, the future of groupware will be the result of practical efforts by users and vendors, regardless of what the forecasters and industry analysts think. In this chapter, we are writing for both users and vendors, but with an emphasis on prospective users.

We begin with scenarios that summarize the lessons derived from earlier chapters in this book. These scenarios provide a vision of specific areas in which use of groupware can make a difference. These are user scenarios in which we emphasize business applications rather than technology per se. Whereas the scenarios in Chapter 6 describe possible industry infrastructures for groupware, these scenarios focus on promising user applications. We are building directly on current user activities, as summarized in Chapter 2, but the scenarios incorporate our judgments regarding high payoff areas that new users should consider. Chapter 2 scenarios emphasize groupware functions; this chapter anticipates future groupware applications.

For each scenario, we provide our judgment regarding target purchasers, target users within the purchasing organizations, types of users who are pursuing the proposed scenario, buying factors perceived by the users, important system capabilities, and potential pitfalls.

These categories form the outline for each of the following scenarios. They are not presented in order of attractiveness, because each approach will have its own strengths and weaknesses in particular situations. All these scenarios are worthy of pursuit by prospective groupware users and vendors.

"THIS ONE WRITES SOME FINE LYRICS, AND THE OTHER ONE HAS COMPOSED SOME BEAUTIFUL MUSIC, BUT THEY JUST DON'T SEEM TO HIT IT OFF AS COLLABORATORS."

SCENARIO 1: THE PROJECT TEAMMATE

This scenario builds directly on the growing importance of business teams. Time and task deadlines are characteristic of the business teams that are attracted to groupware. Geographic distances among team members underscore their communication needs, and the distances need not be great—sometimes different offices in an office park are enough. Look for teams with demanding tasks, good working relationships, and the resources to move quickly.

TARGET PURCHASERS: Directors of R&D or engineering, executives for project-oriented companies (especially in project-oriented industries such as aerospace or construction, and project leaders.

TARGET USERS: Engineers of all types who work on team-oriented projects, computer development teams (hardware or software), other technically oriented teams, and teams that are willing to work through computers, even if the personnel are not technically inclined.

EXAMPLES: Engineering teams for communication among engineers on aircraft construction projects, data-processing teams for software development projects with users at separate locations, military task force teams for brainstorming and idea development, government contractor teams for technical staff working on interrelated tasks, and planning teams for non-profit agencies.

BUYING FACTORS: Better distribution of expertise across organizations, ability to meet seemingly impossible deadlines, competitive advantage (for example, in contract bidding), ability for quick responses to inevitable crises inherent in crash projects, and ability to involve more people on a regular basis.

SYSTEM CAPABILITIES: Audio, text, graphics or other image, access to additional computer capabilities, and use from desktops and conference rooms (synchronous or asynchronous). Optional: motion video, still video.

PITFALLS: Business teams have an intense but often limited lifespan, and the need for a system may go away when the project is over. Thus, system use could die with the project. Also, project teams often have unusual buying patterns and demanding requirements: it is often hard to identify the best buying channels and the right timing.

SCENARIO 2: THE MARKETING EDGE

Marketing and sales teams are often geographically scattered, and many of them are constantly on the move. Yet strong demands exist for updates on new products, competitive offerings, and customer information. Groupware can provide a link for personnel in this intense field, a link that can provide an edge over competitors.

TARGET PURCHASERS: Executives and other leaders of sales and marketing organizations, leaders of decentralized companies such as franchise operations, and telecommunications or information systems planners in companies in which such people work closely with marketing organizations (such companies are rare at present).

TARGET USERS: Marketing and sales personnel, traveling salespeople, and franchise and dealership networks.

EXAMPLES: Salesforces for drug products to allow updates regarding new products and competitive developments; buyers and merchandisers for various department store chains for buying, sales, and inventory control discussions; insurance executives for the sale of large corporate insurance policies; and salesforce linkages via laptop PCs.

BUYING FACTORS: Competitive advantages, reduction of expenses for sales and marketing operations, improved communication with field personnel, decreased need for supervisory personnel, and the ability to provide overnight restructuring of sales-incentive program and customer discounts.

SYSTEM CAPABILITIES: Audio, text, and flexibility in how system can be accessed (for example, portability can be very useful). Store-and-forward is particularly useful because of scheduling problems inherent with these groups. Video is sometimes important; for example, to see new products. Graphics may also be important.

PITFALLS: It is often hard to get the attention of marketing and salespeople, and thus it may be hard to sell them on the advantages of groupware. Competitive pressure will be the most effective drawing card, and a few visible success stories could have a big impact.

SCENARIO 3: THE TRAINING EDGE

Requirements for staff training are intense in many industries, and groupware can provide a cost-effective means for reaching the people who need it. Either small or large group training is possible, either on an intra- or intercompany basis. Teletraining (like training itself) often may be perceived as unexciting, but there is tremendous business need for it at the present time, and the case for groupware can be made very convincing.

TARGET PURCHASERS: Training directors, executives in business areas that have high training needs, organizations that provide training services commercially, and professional organizations that offer training.

TARGET USERS: Trainers; potential trainees in many different fields, but especially in technical fields in which it is imperative to keep up to date; and people with ongoing needs for continuing education or licensing.

EXAMPLES: Vendor teletraining services for key customers, computer-supported private broadcast video systems for internal training, university offerings for statewide continuing education courses, and executive training programs.

BUYING FACTORS: Improved distribution of training resources across large geographic distances, low cost per trainee, easier access to training programs for remotely located employees, and means for catching up with training needs in industries in which training has become critical to business success.

SYSTEM CAPABILITIES: Broadcast video with follow-up audio, graphics, text. Various combinations are possible, given specific requirements of the subject matter involved in the training. A wide range of media is possible—even audio-only networks have proved very successful. Computer-assisted learning applications can also play a big role.

PITFALLS: The training function often is not perceived positively within companies. Also, trainers themselves often are not particularly innovative or open to new ideas. Although training is a current hot item in some companies, it is often perceived as far removed from "real business."

SCENARIO 4: THE PROFESSIONAL'S ASSISTANT

Groupware capabilities can be packaged with services geared toward specific professional groups. Such a vertical-market approach would allow more content-specific services and system capabilities. It also would allow more-precise market segmentation of potential customers.

TARGET PURCHASERS: Managing directors for firms in areas such as architecture, engineering, law, medicine, retailing, and accounting, and small practitioners in these professions.

TARGET USERS: Architects, engineers, lawyers, medical professionals, retail store operators, accountants, and other professionals.

EXAMPLES: Several architectural firms have begun such efforts, as have a range of other professional groups. The activities of professional groups such as electrical engineers (IEEE) suggest the need for such services.

BUYING FACTORS: Professionals, particularly in small organizations, have strong needs to communicate and exchange information with others in topic areas specific to their professions. A "professional's helper" service could provide access to high-quality and low-cost information for individual professionals.

SYSTEM CAPABILITIES: Text, access to computer capabilities, audio, and desktop access. Optional: graphics (especially for graphically oriented professions) or other forms of image.

PITFALLS: Vertically segmented products in the information-technology areas often are difficult to introduce and support with an expert sales staff, particularly across wide geographic areas. Focusing on specific regions may be most appropriate, though this would limit revenue potential. Starting with one or a small number of professions would be most desirable, because the logistics of establishing sales support structures would be imposing.

SCENARIO 5: ACCESS TO ANSWERS

Often, a time-critical piece of information cannot be found, or it resides in a distant location or with an inaccessible person. The person who really has answers often is not at the right place at the right time. An electronic system for improving this matching of questions with answers has clear-cut business value.

POTENTIAL PURCHASERS: Executives or division heads with strong interests in communications within their organizations, telecommunications or information systems planners, and R&D directors.

POTENTIAL USERS: Users could come from varied backgrounds; a key criterion is a need for information that cannot be easily accessed.

EXAMPLES: Government contractor sessions to consult remote experts during briefings in Washington, trouble-shooting systems to allow access to engineering information from remote sites, and project support systems to provide access to technical information.

BUYING FACTORS: For this selling angle to be attractive, a prospective customer must take a broad organizational view of the value of improved communications. Compelling forces will be company-specific but might include the shortening of business cycles, providing better customer service, competitive advantage, and so on. Effects probably will be hard to measure, and thus the need must be compelling enough to override the bean counters.

SYSTEM CAPABILITIES: Expect variations in user requirements here, because motivations and subject matter to be communicated will be customer-specific. Both real-time and store-and-forward media will have roles. Desktop access seems very important. AI capabilities for people and idea matching would be very useful.

PITFALLS: The variations in media requirements and buying factors mean that it is hard to offer a consistent product with a manageable range of options. Also, this product orientation requires a somewhat enlightened purchaser with a broad vision of the organization. Such people often are hard to find, or at least it is hard to find them at times when they have money to spend.

SCENARIO 6: THE ELECTRONIC ORGANIZATION

The vision for sale here is the organization without walls. If reporting chains and key roles can be linked electronically, new types of organizations become possible.

TARGET PURCHASERS: Organizations with extensive computer networks, executives in charge of new business units, executives in charge of decentralized organizations, entrepreneurs who are considering the creation of new businesses, and venture-capital companies investing in new businesses.

TARGET USERS: Colleagues who are geographically separated carrying out different, but interdependent, organizational responsibilities. The specific characteristics of these user vary widely, but they all have to have organizational needs to communicate; teleconferencing would provide a means to make this possible.

EXAMPLES: Private messaging and conferencing systems that allow connections to various other information systems. Various software production groups also fall within this category, most of which have created their own electronic connections. New start-ups that employ electronically distributed staffs using lap computers are also beginning to emerge.

BUYING FACTORS: Competitive advantage, lower operating expenses, flexibility in structuring (or restructuring) of a business, and improved flexibility involving remotely located employees.

SYSTEM CAPABILITIES: The key is store-and-forward, with text, audio, access to computer aids, and deskstop access (or portable) as basics. Options: graphics, image capture.

PITFALLS: Although the electronic organization is a very attractive concept, it is difficult to implement (and thus to sell) quickly. The most likely users may be small, entrepreneurial companies, but this is not an easy market to stake out. Users or vendors who pursue this scenario will definitely be creating a market, at least in the short run.

SCENARIO 7: THE STRATEGIC EDGE

Increasingly, creative use of information technologies is being viewed as a strategic weapon for a company. Such a view implies direct effects on the mission of the organization and the ways its business is conducted. The specifics vary as corporate strategies vary, but the impacts can be profound.

TARGET PURCHASERS: Executives who have strategic responsibility for their organizations and information systems planners in those companies in which these roles participate directly in strategic decisions.

TARGET USERS: Varied, depending on the specific strategy developed.

EXAMPLES: Examples have occurred in the airline, health care, real estate, food, automobile, trucking, and insurance industries. Other examples cut across industries, such as franchising—which is making increasingly heavy use of electronic systems for strategic advantage. Most of these examples are not yet employing groupware capabilities, but this would be a logical next step.

BUYING FACTORS: Direct link to the promise of improvement in corporate position; the specific factors vary greatly, depending on the business of the prospective user. In general, "locking in" customers or "locking out" competitors is a strong incentive.

SYSTEM CAPABILITIES: Varied, depending on specific customer requirements.

PITFALLS: The use of computers as a corporate weapon is a clear direction, but it has also been overhyped. Specific strategic options often need to be developed to identify prospective applications. User-vendor "partnerships" will be very important. The current problem is translating the Strategic Edge scenario from a consultant truism into specific business opportunities. It may be that it is more of an approach to the other scenarios described than a separate scenario in itself.

ACROSS THE SCENARIOS

In the 17 scenarios in Chapter 2, the emphasis is on system functionality from a user point of view, each representing a different angle on groupware functionality. The scenarios overlap considerably, because they are different interpretations of the core groupware concept. In Chapter 6, the nine scenarios focus on possible industry structures for the delivery of groupware products and services.

The scenarios in this final chapter pick up elements of both the Chapter 2 and Chapter 6 scenarios, but the emphasis is on the business value being provided by groupware, rather than system functionality or groupware industry structure. In fact, real-world examples of groupware success will be more specific than these scenarios. For example, Project Teammate will appear as the use of groupware by a specific business team, with an emphasis on that team's accomplishments rather than the capabilities of groupware. The Marketing

Edge example will be an approach to sales success with details about particular sales teams. A few innovative user organizations will recognize the value of encouraging groupware use across business teams in various parts of the company or across companies, but most of the emphasis will be on specific business situations, rather than groupware per se. Groupware functionalities, and the systems people who support them, will be behind-the-scenes performers.

The scenarios in this chapter provide a starting point for uncovering or creating such business opportunities within an organization. They should be the stimulus for this search, rather than a rigid set of criteria to be matched.

GENERATING NEW GROUPWARE IDEAS

These scenarios are only a beginning, based on what we have seen in our research on groupware thus far. It is also important for prospective users to generate their own groupware application ideas. This section suggests a simple framework for generating groupware application ideas growing out of the ideas developed in this book, particularly in Chapter 5, "Softer Software." Figure 20 contains two

FIGURE 20

A Framework for Generating Groupware Application Ideas

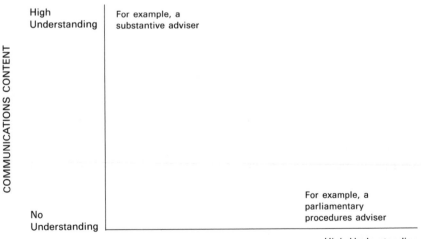

GROUP PROCESS

axes: process and content. *Process* refers to the interpersonal process of conducting a group communications session, encompassing everything from the process of initiating communications connections to the group process sustained during an actual meeting. *Content* refers to the actual content being discussed within a group.

Each axis is arrayed between *high understanding* and *no understanding*. The further out an application is along an axis, the more closely its use depends on the hypothetical groupware system understanding of either content (vertical axis) or process (horizontal axis). For example, a groupware idea located at the top right of the chart would have to have high understanding of both the process of the communication being performed and its content.

The degree of sensitivity to both the content and the process required of a groupware system can dramatically affect its practicality of implementation, given current technology. In general, the more focused and structured a problem domain is and the less connected it is to other external domains (particularly things involving common sense), the more likely it is that it can be effectively represented in a computer program. Expressed in another way, computers find it easy to accomplish tasks people find difficult (such as calculating out to a hundred decimals), but difficult or impossible to perform tasks people find trivial (such as understanding the difference between the words *through* and *threw* when spoken).

In general, products that require comprehensive understanding along either axis are more difficult to implement than those that do not. Products that require comprehensive understanding on both axes are probably not achievable in the short run. It is possible, however, to push a significant distance toward the outside edge without entering the realm of impossibility, especially if one is working within a formal environment (say, work tasks involving petroleum engineers in a specific content area). In addition to restricting application to formal environments, one could also avoid the impossibility trap by restricting the bandwidth the product operates within; for example, it will be much easier to implement a groupware product in which the user must communicate by typing on a terminal than one in which the product must first translate the user's spoken words.

At the other extreme, groupware systems that can be successful while reflecting high levels of ignorance in both content and process are often easy to implement (they require no AI technology), and many have been implemented. Most of today's teleconferencing products fit within this category, clustering toward the lower left of the figure. These existing applications are of particular interest for groupware prospectors, by asking the question "How could these products be enhanced by the addition of groupware capabilities?" it may be possible to create new, more capable products from old.

A pattern quickly emerges here. Moving from the lower left to the upper right of the chart generally reflects a movement from products already existing to products impossible to implement today. This is not to say that a product at the upper right cannot be developed, but rather that its development cycle will be longer. We are arguing that the most interesting opportunities lie at the outside edge of existing products and that implementation is made more possible by utilization of AI spin-off technologies (as discussed in Chapter 5).

In our work we have employed a number of methods for generating groupware application ideas. One of the most successful is a matrix of AI concepts (Chapter 5) and groupware scenarios (Chapter 2), as depicted in Table 12. Brainstorming sessions for possible groupware ideas that might arise out of each intersection are often fruitful.

These frameworks are intended to be suggestive rather than all-inclusive. We have found them useful in our work, but other approaches to idea generation may work better for others. The important point to realize is that there are many groupware ideas yet to be created.

GUIDELINES

The groupware application scenarios in this chapter, coupled with additional ideas generated with the preceding exercises, lead to a range of groupware options for prospective users and vendors to consider. Prospective users should look for overlaps among these scenarios and important aspects of their own organizations. Vendors should review the pros and cons of each scenario, considering their own strengths and weaknesses. For vendors, the argument for concentrating one's resources is strong. The alternative is to spread oneself thinly across what is still a small market. A concentrated approach is likely to be more successful in creating markets, even if they begin as niches. Groupware, like all emerging technologies, needs some big wins early in the game. Selling applications is critical in this quest for dramatic successes, and this book has suggested

Table 12 GROUPWARE IDEA GENERATION GRID

USER SCENARIOS	Automated Programming	Robotics	Computer Vision	Knowledge Media	Natural Language Understanding	Natural Language Generation	Expert Systems	Inheritance	Agents	WYSIWIS	Hypermedia
1. Facilitation Services											
2. Decision Support											
3. Telephone Extension											
4. Presentation Software											
5. Project Management											
6. Calendaring											
7. Group Writing											
8. Beyond White Board											
9. Screen Sharing											
0. Computer Conferencing											
1. Text Filtering											
2. Teleconference Aid											
3. Conversation Structuring											
4. Memory Management											
5. Spontaneous Interaction											
6. Comprehensive Support											
7. Nonhuman Participants											

where to begin. For users, the option of trying several small-scale efforts is appealing.

Looking across the scenarios, it is possible to identify some rules of thumb that apply to both users and vendors, a kind of checklist for considering and introducing groupware.

Positioning—The First Step

Positioning of groupware (or whatever it is called) is important. This is a basic marketing concept that is too often overlooked. Few people want to buy a mysterious concept or black box. Vendors need to provide potential buyers with a product concept that is easily understood and reasonably focused, rather than the chameleon tactics currently favored by some vendors. Even within user organizations, positioning of groupware will be critical to its success.

Know Your Needs and Wants

Needs assessment for groupware is likely to be tricky, because most users will not understand what groupware is or what it could do for them. Such problems, however, are no excuse for ignoring needs assessment. What it takes is a creative and flexible approach to understanding key business needs, as well as things people want to do but do not know how to do. Some education can be built into a needs-assessment process to introduce prospective users to the functions that groupware might provide, without overwhelming them with technical details.

A good rule of thumb is to look for current pains or problems—roadblocks to getting the job done. Beyond pains, "critical success factors" interviewing can be done to identify those things that must be done right for an organization to succeed. In short, needs assessment for groupware is delicate, but the result—picking the best early applications—is well worth the effort.[1]

Users as Individuals

One should not assume that all users are the same, or that there is one "right person" to talk with about groupware. If, for example, a product is positioned as a sales tool, it is more appropriate to start with the marketing or sales department. End-user support can be a powerful aid. In the short run, groupware products and services often will be purchased directly by end users.

The successful vendor should learn enough about the prospective user organization to know who is doing what, by doing as much research beforehand as possible and trying to understand its culture. Note that successful groupware users often succeed because there is a champion in the company. Who might this person be? Generally, the vendor or internal system person must look for someone with planning and purchasing responsibilities, an innovative thinker with some influence in the organization. It may be the same person who first bought PCs or who recommended a state-of-the-art telephone system to replace an antiquated system. Once such people have a visceral commitment to groupware, the company sell becomes much easier. Vendors are not the only ones who will have to sell; the early users also will have to sell groupware internally.

Applications Are Key

Few vendors, according to nonusers and users, take the time to learn enough about a prospective user organization to determine appropriate applications. Understanding the corporate culture is important. Does the company have a lot of meetings among people from different offices? Do people travel instead of telephoning? Are most contacts with people inside or outside the organization? Are contacts more formal or informal? Do a lot of memos circulate throughout the company? How about graphic or numerical data? How *do* people communicate internally? Understanding the communications process should lead to a promising groupware application.

One key to convincing potential customers is education, a word that vendors use often when discussing sales to nonusers. But the people who most often need educating are the vendors. Potential customers are not likely to become excited about an unknown product, particularly one that does not provide a solution to any obvious problem or directly save money. The key to a sale is understanding the customer's situation—focusing on an organization, doing a needs analysis, determining where groupware might be used and what it could accomplish.

There is a serious difference of perception here: most vendors think of themselves as applications oriented. In our research, we have found that they are not perceived that way at all by users. And, of course, users must understand their own potential groupware applications before they can explain those needs to vendors.

Fit the Existing Technology

An emphasis on applications must be complemented by a technology fit. More and more customers have offices that feature a variety of electronic devices. Even if the term office automation is passe, the concept is not. The customer will feel infinitely more comfortable with a groupware product if it is compatible with or can be used by existing computers, the PBX system, and whatever other electronic aids are around. The physical requirements of groupware must be addressed in relation to the customer's situation; for example, additional cabling or an extra set of wires in everyone's office may not be feasible. Vendors must work within the constraints of the existing office environment.

Sweeteners from Vendors

Once the needs of an organization are understood, it is reasonable for new users to expect some sweeteners. Vendors can, for example, provide a no-obligation, risk-free demonstration; install the product on a trial basis, if possible; train potential users; promote the product within the organization; be available for questions or assistance; track results, both tangible and intangible; provide the potential customer with hard facts showing the value of the product in that organization. Of course, there will be some groupware providers who do not have the resources to offer such incentives, but there is no harm in asking.

Do Not Forget User Incentives

The decision to *purchase* groupware products may be distinctly different from the decision to *use* groupware products. Too often with emerging information technologies, system enthusiasts have forgotten that what is good for the company is not always perceived as good by individual employees. Table 13 displays this distinction in types of incentives. Most vendors think long and hard about incentives to get companies to purchase a system. It is the "second sell," however, that is the one most often underemployed: How to create incentives for people to use groupware products once they are available. Will groupware help relieve their personal work pains? Will groupware provide any new perks? What industry analyst Rich Harkness of Boeing Information Services has called "end user self-interest" plays a critical (though often unrecognized) role in the success or failure of new systems. (Harkness is an excellent source of such insights, because he had long experience in the marketing of

Table 13   INCENTIVES TO USE A NEW SYSTEM

PERSONAL INCENTIVES

CORPORATE INCENTIVES	LO	HI
LO		Example: Personal Computers
HI	Example: Video Teleconferencing	

video teleconferencing before he joined Boeing.) Special effort should be made to ensure that groupware is attractive to the individual users who will use it, not just the company that employs them.

The Importance of Service Support

One radical tactic that vendors (both external and internal) might pursue is to treat their current customers very nicely. Users complain of difficulties with vendors: poor service, for example, or inability to talk to anyone who can quickly help resolve problems. Many vendors are simply not very responsive to customers. The more sophisticated the system, the more likely there are to be problems. Users are concerned about maintaining their system, and so they often are forced to use nonvendor services to keep their systems going. Vendors bemoan the lack of success stories, but there will not *be* any success stories unless the vendors are able to satisfy their customers. Unfortunately and ironically, successful vendors sometimes become too successful to meet the needs of their ongoing customers. Many of the most effective groupware efforts in the short run will be the result of partnerships between users and vendors.

Develop Case Studies

Early experience with groupware can reveal important lessons about what works (and what does not work) in a particular organization. Too often, in the heat of the moment, these early experiences go undocumented or underutilized. Learning is not transferred to others, and even the success stories go untold. Special effort should be made that the early experiences—both successes and failures—are carefully evaluated and the results shared.

Is It Working?

Evaluation of the effects of groupware use can easily be forgotten or postponed until it is too late to measure them. Pre- and post-use measures are basic to systematic evaluation of effects, and even these approaches are difficult when "soft" effects are involved. Business team performance is sometimes measurable, sometimes not. Drawing causal links to the effects of groupware is likely to be difficult. It will be worth the effort, though, when management asks the telling question: "Is it working?" In such situations, it often matters little that current methods (before groupware was introduced) have not been evaluated and may not qualify according to the same criteria being used to evaluate the new way of working.

The introduction of groupware over the next three years will not be for the faint of heart. There will be many struggles as groupware tools come out of the shell. But the opportunities are real.

Business teams provide a powerful vision of organizations that can act with speed, efficiency, and effectiveness. Groupware can make the vision of business teams a reality.

APPENDIX A

Groupware Lessons from the Teleconferencing Market

ROBERT JOHANSEN AND JEFF CHARLES

Teleconferencing is used broadly here: interactive group communications through any electronic medium or mix of media. The primary media are motion video, graphics, audio, and text. (Unfortunately, the popular business press has tended to define teleconferencing more narrowly to mean only video teleconferencing.) Both two-way video and point-to-multipoint video, often called *Business TV,* are included in our definition of teleconferencing.

Most forms of teleconferencing have been offered as products for at least five years, although those variants that build on the PC are more recent. The oldest industry trade show in teleconferencing, Telecon (organized by Applied Business Telecommunications in San Ramon, California), has been going on for nearly 10 years. The International Teleconferencing Association (ITCA) of McLean, Virginia, an industry association of users and vendors, was founded in 1983. ITCA has over 500 members and attracts over 2,000 people to its major trade show.

Experience with teleconferencing in the marketplace has been mixed, ranging from resounding success to outright failure. Conference calling is the largest portion of the market right now, followed by Business TV, in which a motion video signal is sent out to many sites, with audio feedback for questions or comments. Other forms of teleconferencing have been successful for specific types of applications.

Teleconferencing offers communication support for teams, in a similar fashion to the computer support offered by groupware.

Note: This chapter draws from and updates previous IFTF market research on teleconferencing, particularly that conducted as part of the Outlook Project—a joint venture with TeleSpan of Altadena, California. Elliot Gold of TeleSpan contributed greatly to the ideas in this section.

Therefore, those interested in groupware should look closely at experiences with teleconferencing—both positive and negative. We begin with an overview of one of the most successful applications of teleconferencing to date, one involving marketing and sales. Next, we explore the dark side—teleconferencing failures. If the lessons of teleconferencing can be learned, we feel that the growth of groupware will be accelerated greatly.

TELECONFERENCING SUCCESSES

Teleconferencing success stories have varied from strategic to routine. Strategic applications are those that directly affect the direction of the company. They include applications that make money; raise money; manage a major deal, merger, or acquisition; or respond speedily to a crisis situation that could affect company profitability, image, or both. Routine success stories are based on applications that relate to increased efficiency (due to teleconferencing) in day-to-day operations, such as project work, project reviews, and staff meetings, usually accompanied by significant travel avoidance and savings of personal time. But of all the success stories to date, one subset stands out—user applications in the general area of marketing. We concentrate on that in the next few pages.

Marketing applications of teleconferencing encompass a variety of activities. The basic four Ps of marketing are product, place, promotion, and price. Product includes product quality, features, options, and style. Place encompasses distribution channels and related issues. Price is self-explanatory. Generally, product, place, and price do not lend themselves very well to teleconferencing. The fourth P, promotion, is a different matter. Promotion, which includes advertising, sales, and other forms of publicity, is the focus of this "teleconferencing for profit" discussion. Moreover, we concentrate on marketing to specific market segments (business, education, and government), and not individual consumers.

Fortunately, most customers admit that marketing belongs in their organization, whether or not they do it systematically. The job of a teleconferencing provider is to understand the role of marketing in a user organization and then to demonstrate how teleconferencing can complement or supplement the marketing process. A summary of these opportunities—those now present, and those that will be here soon—follows.

The major thrusts in today's teleconferencing marketplace come from room-to-room video, desk-to-desk audio, and multipoint video. Room-to-room video is expensive—for equipment, for transmission costs, and very often for room construction. Because operating costs are high, meetings are usually better planned and shorter than face-to-face meetings. This often proves advantageous to participants, because a lot of material can be compressed into the meeting. Room-to-room video is growing, albeit more slowly than expected. The driving force enabling that growth is the declining cost of transmission and video coder/decoders (called *codecs*) needed to transmit the video image in digital form. Further, there is now a growing installed base of over 500 two-way video rooms in North America, permitting companies with compatible codecs to interconnect to cities where they do not now have private rooms.

The successful applications are coming from aerospace, banking, insurance, and retailing companies. The applications range from the use of video teleconferencing for enabling the successful relocation of computer programmers (Aetna Life and Casualty) to job interviewing (an aerospace company) to management budget reviews (Sears). Teleconferencing encompasses a wide range of costs for equipment, from under $100 for a desktop audio conferencing unit to hundreds of thousands of dollars for some full-motion video rooms.

Desk-to-Desk Teleconferencing

Desk-to-desk audio teleconferencing is generally less formal than room-to-room teleconferencing. Transmission time is cheap and available on demand, and the equipment is at hand; thus it is relatively easy to have an ad hoc meeting. Such "conference calling" is a normal part of many businesses, though it is often not called teleconferencing. Because of its convenience, the applications span many industrial sectors, both in manufacturing and service industries. Airlines use conference calls routinely for management consultations and coordination of dispersed operations. Pharmaceutical companies use it for training, product assessments, and staff meetings. Banks are using it for investment coordination internationally, and a variety of higher educational institutions are taking advantage of the ease and versatility of audioconferences for crisis meetings—

such as strikes—when they need speedy and immediate decisions on urgent issues during crises.

Business TV

Lately, another form of teleconferencing has become popular, Business TV, used for presentations or company-wide meetings. Video is broadcast from one site to many sites; the viewers have an audio connection to the teleconference. At the end of 1986, 41 networks broadcasted to over 5,500 receiving sites. By 1987, the number expanded to over 50 networks and 11,000 reception sites. Companies using business television include Hewlett-Packard, J.C. Penney, Eastman Kodak, Merrill Lynch, and Texas Instruments. Hewlett-Packard now has built video into its marketing and product strategy, satisfied that business television helps to sell its products. The Automotive Satellite TV Network transmits daily programming to car dealers. Such industry networks are increasing.

THE INTERSECTION OF MARKETING
AND TELECONFERENCING

Teleconferencing is a tool that sparks considerable interest among marketing people. After all, marketing people are always looking for new ways to reach their customers. Although market research has become extremely sophisticated, promotional marketing has changed slowly. Teleconferencing can bring marketing promotion into the computer age.

A quick analysis of the different components of marketing communications indicates that teleconferencing has the most value in specific aspects of personal selling. Teleconferencing can also aid sales promotion and publicity. Its role in helping an organization's advertising efforts is less significant. Personal selling is particularly important in selling industrial goods and services, particularly big-ticket items. Advertising is generally much less critical in the marketing mix for these kinds of items. Figure 21 shows the zone in which teleconferencing has proven most valuable.

Marketing provides a new set of applications that are also new to the teleconferencing field. Once, not so long ago, teleconferencing was a typical high-tech sale; that is, products and services were devel-

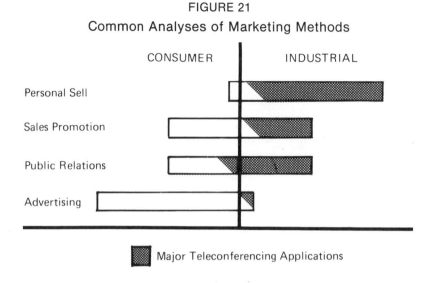

FIGURE 21

Common Analyses of Marketing Methods

oped without a clear vision of their function within a user organization. No one spent much time thinking about target customers. The philosophy was simple: engineer a good product and people will buy it.

The technology argument is no longer a good means of making a sale. Indeed, it has become even less workable as people become more technologically sophisticated. Customers want tools, not puzzles. Before they will spend much money on teleconferencing, they want to understand not just how it works and what it does, but what they can use it for and what impact is it likely to have on their work and the organization. This is especially true for the high-ticket teleconferencing items. And it is not just whether it can save them money. The big question they want answered is "How can teleconferencing move my business forward?"

All companies market, but many do so inefficiently. When teleconferencing comes to be viewed as a marketing tool, there are some immediate implications:

All medium or large companies have a marketing group, and thus they become potential teleconferencing users.

Those who would like to introduce teleconferencing have a better idea of what people to approach in a user organization.

Marketing directly affects total revenues, not just cost savings.

Marketing, by the way, is not just an external operation. Electronic meetings are often well suited to internal promotion efforts such as informing employees about a new development or project or generating enthusiasm for a new venture. Federal Express, for example, holds regular ''family briefings'' for all employees and their families via video teleconferencing. Teleconferencing can also be used more conventionally to coordinate marketing efforts within a company. Hewlett Packard does precisely that for its domestic as well as international sales force.

SURE WINNERS

A few types of marketing applications of teleconferencing are already proven winners.

Sure Winner One: Supporting the Reps

We have noted that the most commonly used method of selling big-ticket products—and the most costly marketing tool—is a sales representative calling on a customer. Often, however, a presentation by a rep is disappointing to the prospective customer. Although a face-to-face meeting usually has the advantage of establishing a positive rapport between the rep and the prospective client, in many cases it simply cannot provide the client with an adequate understanding of the product.

A teleconference held in conjunction with a personal sales pitch can greatly enhance the value of the representative's visit to a prospective customer. For example, a customer who is interested in a piece of heavy machinery could participate in a full-motion video teleconference. During the teleconference, the customer can watch and talk to people who are manufacturing or operating the machinery; they can ask questions and see a complete demonstration of the equipment's capabilities. This reduces the lead time required for a sale, eliminates the risky role of the sales representative as go-between, and gives the customer a greater sense of ease. Note that this application probably does not eliminate travel, because the sales rep still visits and the customer inevitably will want to see the equipment in person before actually purchasing it. But it does complement and extend the value of travel.

Examples of companies using teleconferencing for supporting their reps include:

Hewlett-Packard: A point-to-multipoint video teleconference network has been created for new product introductions and similar activities, greatly increasing the resources available to sales reps.

Merrill Lynch: A sales rep in this context is a stock broker. Merrill Lynch has provided point-to-multipoint video teleconferences that provide up-to-the-minute information about topics relevant to investors. Brokers and customers are present for the broadcasts, with the brokers available to talk business after the teleconference.

Hoffman-La Roche: Drug sales reps are dependent on accurate information about new drugs as they are introduced. Hoffman-La Roche uses audio teleconferencing, supplemented by slides and background information, to do briefings on new drug products and to discuss issues important to the field reps.

Apple Computer: AppleLink is a computer-based system that links Apple with its dealers. Account reps use the system to stay in regular touch with dealers between in-person visits. The system supports the reps by making product and service information available instantly to the dealers. This is not a conventional teleconferencing system, but it is similar and it is suggestive of many other possibilities.

J.C. Penney: National buyers use full-motion video to sell new fashions to regional buyers and retailers all over the United States. The models show the clothes on the video, and buyers order on the spot, cutting the long process of on-site road shows, order entry by mail, and delivery by several weeks. Fairweather, an upscale women's clothing merchandiser in Canada, uses audio conferencing to coordinate similar advertising and sales activities.

Sure Winner Two: Trade Shows

Trade shows provide another opportunity to use teleconferencing for marketing. It is often impossible to demonstrate a product or service at a trade show if it is difficult to transport it. The product may not travel well, or it may be too bulky or too fragile to use in a trade show exhibit. The nature of many services makes it inherently difficult to display them at a trade show.

There are many examples of teleconferencing used to market at a trade show. Here are a few:

An office furniture show can feature a teleconference with engineers discussing design processes, a discussion with potential customers about possible design changes, and a demonstration of people using new office furniture.

For a travel agents' conference, a meeting with tour agents in distant cities can be conducted. Colorful brochures and taped video presentations can substitute for these teleconference applications, of course, but they can never replace the valuable interactions of a live teleconference.

Conference speakers can appear via teleconference. In this way, the conference organizer may be able to obtain a prominent speaker who would otherwise be unable to travel to the meeting.

Many specific industries have begun to use teleconferencing in conjunction with trade shows: CDN (computer trade shows) and HSN (hospital trade shows), for example. In each case, teleconferencing is used to extend the audience and to broaden the appeal of the trade show.

At the ITCA's May 1987 conference, British Telecom took the opportunity of advertising its multisite conferencing unit (MCU) by giving a demonstration of a five-nation hookup on the equipment. Industry experts and telecommunications agencies (also called PTTs) from London, Paris, Amsterdam, Bonn, and Washington, D.C., were linked on the videoconference. The MCU at British Telecom's International Videoconferencing Gateway exchange in London acted as the automatic switch between all five sites. The ITCA conference marked the first commercial use of the equipment for an international videoconference.

Sure Winner Three: Sales Training

Similar to Sure Winner One, this application focuses on the training and educational aspects of sales. Particularly in high-tech industries, the sales staff must have up-to-date information. In most cases, however, the sales staff is spread out across the country or the world.

Bringing them together in one place at one time is either unwieldy, expensive, or (most commonly) both.

Examples of companies using teleconferencing for sales training include:

Deere & Company: In the heat of industry crises, Deere & Company began using audio teleconferencing and voice mail to train its international sales staff. Both product and competitive information are included.

IBM: To provide ongoing courses to their training sites for sales staff (as well as others), IBM created their (ISEN) network. The system includes point-to-multi-point video, audio controlled by the instructor, and a polling mechanism for use with question-and-answer sessions.

AT&T: The Cincinnati-based AT&T National Teletraining Center runs daily lunchtime training sessions via audio for sales staff as well as more structured sessions in specific contact areas. Over 200 locations are involved, with a broad mix of teleconferencing media. Tens of thousands of people each year now attend these sessions, with very strong positive results.

Digital Equipment Corporation: To train its 8,000 sales support personnel throughout North America with important, time-sensitive business announcements, Digital used its own network plus hotel sites in the United States and Canada. To reach Digital's sales people out in the field would have required up to two months using conventional media, the company estimates.

Sure Winner Four: Splashy Events

In the marketing world, extravaganzas attract attention, and sometimes it is the kind of attention that sells products. Teleconferencing can be used with flair to create a splashy marketing event. For example, Texas Instruments began holding one-day, point-to-multipoint video briefings on AI in November of 1985. The teleconference was free to attendees and was promoted as an introduction for business people trying to understand and profit from AI. Texas Instruments was able to position itself instantly as a leader in AI by virtue of organizing this teleconference. It connected 448 sites for viewing only, set up 28 locations with the option for telephone questions to the presenters, and had the show carried by 12 cable television links. In all, more than 30,000 people saw the show. Texas Instruments was so pleased with the result that it held a second such teleconference which was viewed by 50,000 people at 850 locations in 16 countries. Follow-ups have continued to expand on these early efforts.

The Texas Instruments experience provides a textbook lesson in the use of teleconferencing for marketing, through the use of single splashy events. Before the teleconferences, Texas Instruments was not very visible in the AI world (certainly, several other computer companies had more customer recognition). Now, at least in the minds of many viewers, it is synonymous with AI.

Other businesses have made clever use of splashy events for their marketing advantage, including Southwestern Bell, Johnson & Johnson, and Federal Express. Curiously, religious groups have been very skilled in organizing splashy marketing events (although they typically use more heavenly terminology than "marketing"). Indeed, some of the largest point-to-multipoint video teleconferences have been run by religious groups. Other nonprofit organizations have also taken advantage of this medium, including "Beyond War" (one of the most impressive international gatherings ever), numerous alumni groups doing fund raising, and even national political parties.

Sure Winner Five: Word-of-Mouth Groups

The most subtle of our Sure Winners—at the opposite extreme from the splashy events—is the word-of-mouth group. In some industries, the introduction process for new products is more informal than formal, more ripple than splash. For example, new drug products typically are introduced to medical doctors through a combination of formal and informal means. Although formal product announcements are important, getting doctors to spread the word to other doctors is what really makes a new drug product take off. Some drug companies, such as Hoffman-La Roche, are using teleconferencing to hurry this word-of-mouth process along. At least two independent market research companies have emerged (TeleSession in New York City and Market Navigation in Orangeburg, New York) that specialize in running focus groups by audio teleconference. With a specially adapted bridge, focus groups of medical doctors participate in conference calls that discuss new drugs and the experiences the doctors have had using them. Market Navigation has found that the doctors actually enjoy these meetings and see great value in them. Such word-of-mouth marketing, of course, works best for good products—a drug company paying for a teleconference has little control over what is said about its product.

Word-of-mouth marketing is geared toward the small-group forms of teleconferencing, especially conference calls and—to a lesser extent—computer conferencing. A personal and informal mood has to be established, one in which the word can get out to others.

In the marketing applications of teleconferencing, it is clear that four industries stand out as leaders:

1. High-tech (such as IBM, Hewlett-Packard, and Texas Instruments)
2. Financial services (such as Hambrecht & Quist, Merrill Lynch, and Century 21)
3. Medical (such as the American Hospital Association, the Pacific Presbyterian Medical Center, the American Hospital Network, the Ministry of Health in Canada, and many private hospitals)
4. Retailing (such as J.C. Penney, Sears, and Fairweather)

The following guidelines emerge from these success stories for identifying promising applications:

Look for a geographically distributed salesforce.

Look for places in which a high information need exists, either for salespeople or for customers.

Look for a competitive climate that will encourage innovation.

Look for a willingness to take some risks, because teleconferencing still involves a few changes from the ways of the past.

THOSE WHO SAID NO

In spite of the success stories, teleconferencing is still not a large market. Why is this so? What lessons can be learned that might apply to groupware?

To explore the *problems* of introducing teleconferencing, we interviewed 22 *Fortune* companies that were similar in profile to telecon-

Table 14 INDUSTRY AFFILIATIONS OF COMPANIES

Financial services	7
Consumer products and services	6
General industrial	5
Extraction/refining	4

ference users, but that had *not* become regular users. The nonusers we interviewed all worked for companies that were well established and relatively sophisticated—they were aware of teleconferencing and, in most cases, had dabbled in it. The companies were like the proverbial fish who nibbles at the bait but refuses to swallow the hook. Audio was okay, they thought, for occasional use. Video looked like a lot of fun, but it was perceived as costing too much money. Many of the telecommunications managers who talked about teleconferencing in their organizations seemed to feel that introducing a successful, full-scale teleconferencing system would require overcoming a substantial amount of deep-seated opposition.

Although the number of companies in our informal survey was small (22), they ranged across a broad spectrum (see Table 14). Although the backgrounds of the interviewees were diverse, they had many features in common.

Nearly all of them worked in the telecommunications departments of major organizations. Therefore, they were not primarily involved in planning corporate strategy, nor were they the end users in the company. Most had some autonomy in day-to-day operations, however (see Table 15).

Their organizations all had adequate resources to devote to developing a large-scale teleconferencing network. Many (13) had actually investigated such a network and had decided not to install one for various reasons discussed later.

Their companies were not dissimilar from those organizations that

Table 15 DEGREE OF DECENTRALIZATION IN RESPONDENT COMPANIES[a]

	Mean	Mode	Range
Decentralized management	6.0	7/8	2–10
Decentralized project work	6.7	7/8	1–10
$N = 22$			

[a]Scale of 1–10; 10 = very decentralized.

have whole-heartedly adopted teleconferencing. The corporate culture was not necessarily more restrictive, nor was the organization unreceptive to new ideas. The differences were subtle.

Cost is the main objection many of the respondents gave when asked about the lack of a major teleconferencing system in their organization. Although they understood that teleconferencing encompasses a variety of media, ultimately they seemed to feel (erroneously, as we have pointed out) that teleconferencing equates with full-motion video. And the price tag on full-motion video is just a little too high.

These companies, being well established and relatively stable, tend to have standardized purchasing procedures. All the respondents were familiar with purchasing processes at their organizations, and all but a few said that telecommunications equipment was planned for and purchased by one central department, although exceptions could be made for small-ticket items (see Table 16). Any meaningful purchase, whether included in the budget or not, generally had to be approved by a higher, central authority. Approval inevitably is predicated on the purchaser's justifying the item, usually by proving that it is essential to continuing operations, that it will save money, that it will increase revenues, or that it will improve productivity. A full-scale teleconferencing system is often difficult to justify under these conditions.

Nevertheless, most of these companies had dabbled in teleconferencing, although their experimentation generally was limited to the common loudspeaking telephones. Table 17 shows the types of teleconferencing systems tried. Most of the audio use, as might be expected, has been for ongoing meetings, such as staff meetings, project management, and other regularly scheduled events. The few video uses were all for special, ad hoc events; none of the nonusers had rooms installed. Two of the respondents had participated in a trial of freeze-frame teleconferencing.

In asking why the company had not adopted teleconferencing, we elicited some reactions that were based on subjective, rather than

Table 16   TELECOMMUNICATIONS PLANNING AND PURCHASING
IN RESPONDENT COMPANIES

Totally centralized	14
Department request, approval centralized	3
Departments purchase up to limited amount	2
Decentralized	3

Table 17   TELECONFERENCING MEDIA

System Type	Number
Audio	12
Ad hoc video	3
Freeze frame	2
Audiographics	2
Facsimile	2
Computer	1

Note: Seventeen respondents had tried some kind of conferencing; five of them had tried two kinds.

objective, factors. When queried about levels of satisfaction, most of the respondents expressed contentment with their audio-conferencing experiences, although there were a few complaints about specific pieces of equipment. The only interviewees who voiced real dissatisfaction were those who had used more complicated forms of teleconferencing. One of the freeze-frame users stated that their system was constantly crashing, although the other freeze-frame test participant was generally pleased with the system and saved a substantial amount of money in the travel budget during the period of the trial. A former audiographics user explained that it was difficult to organize a system in a geographically diffused decentralized organization; developing appropriate applications was virtually impossible. Another user of several media, including audiographic and facsimile, gave several reasons for lack of success: poor promotion of the system within the organization, improper control, lack of user awareness, and a dearth of education and training. The initial users of teleconferencing, according to this respondent, had not been chosen wisely.

Is it possible for a nonuser to become a user? After talking to these 22 individuals, we believe that the answer is a qualified yes. The reasons for failure were similar to the standard arguments that people give for not installing teleconferencing, with one significant exception: cost is probably not as important as many people think. In fact, when cost has been an issue, it always seems to be as a plus, a cost savings. Apparently cost is of major concern during the justification phase but becomes less of an issue once the system is operational.

The primary reason for lack of success in the nonuser organizations has been attitudinal: failing to break down the barriers against teleconferencing. "There's no emotional appeal," said one respondent about audio. Users may feel uncomfortable with the system. "People need help and preparation," another respondent said.

Significantly, in many of these cases a vendor had successfully completed the first few steps and had installed an actual system. At that point, the sales mechanism failed. The system never really "caught on" in the company. No one factor is to blame, but it is clear that vendors can and should assume substantial responsibility for keeping a system going through education, promotion, and support.

A critical failure point for teleconferencing that several respondents mentioned was the loss of the major teleconferencing advocate within the organization. "The manager (who had proposed and operated the system) left the company and the division itself was sold off." (This respondent was not sure what had happened to the equipment—it had either been sold or warehoused.) Without the strong and vocal support of at least one relatively senior manager, teleconferencing does not have a chance of succeeding. (Vendors might want to avoid the strong risk of losing a company advocate by ensuring that there are several advocates, including an end user and the telecommunications manager.)

Those Who Considered Teleconferencing

When asked whether they had investigated installing a full-scale teleconferencing system, 13 said that they had. All had rejected the idea. Why? Answers fell into three categories: costs, attitudes, and miscellaneous:

Cost-Related

"Full-motion video was too much."

"When costs of earth stations come down and compression gets better, we might put it in between two or three sites."

"To make video cost effective, we would have to save 40% of travel."

"Much too expensive, period (full motion)."

"Couldn't sell it to senior management—they don't believe in putting out a lot of money for *soft benefits*—they want to see hard dollar savings."

Attitudes

"Attitudes were ambivalent—they wanted full motion but loved to travel."

"Executives like to sit down and look someone in the eye and ask why business isn't producing."

"It was too artificial."

Miscellaneous

"There is no single vendor who can put in the local loops, and so on, for the systems we would need."

"Scheduled a demo and the vendor never showed."

There are few surprises here—this is the kind of resistance that has existed since teleconferencing was first introduced in the market-place.

The most interesting finding was that these nonusers are not os-triches in the teleconferencing world. They are aware of industry de-velopments, and many of them have evaluated teleconferencing for use in their own companies. A few had been involved in teleconfer-encing applications with previous employers. Yet, it is difficult to make teleconferencing fit into their own organization. Apart from the internal problems of dealing with management, negotiating for teleconferencing in the budget, and overcoming user resistance, they are leery of teleconferencing—mostly, full-motion video teleconfer-encing. The major discontent focuses on one external factor, the ven-dor. Although these nonusers were *not* asked about their attitudes toward vendors, because it was assumed that their contacts with ven-dors had been minimal, several expressed the opinion that the ven-dors—not a lack of user acceptance—were responsible for their dis-satisfaction with teleconferencing. "The market is selective and until vendors realize that, they will forever market to the wrong group," said one nonuser. Translation: no vendor had developed appropriate applications for this nonuser. Not everyone wants the same features and the same system. A clothing manufacturer who has targeted the market as inadequately as many teleconferencing vendors do would not stay in business long.

Another nonuser lambasted the attitudes of vendors. According to this respondent, the average vendor spiel goes like this: "We've got a great system for you! If *you* use Amalgamated Widget for the cameras, if *you* call X for earth stations, if *you* call Y for codecs, and *you* guys pioneer the system." What potential user wants to bother assembling a system *and* being a guinea pig? Not this interviewee. (Unfortunately, too many users do follow this procedure to get their system going.) The nonuser added, "If you have a proven product, on the other hand, I might be interested." One tough customer simply did not like the approach that most vendors take. "I can't imagine anything happening based on a telephone contact by a vendor. If someone finally had the persistence to bang down my door to determine the applicability of it here, I'd talk to them." A take-it-or-leave-it attitude is not an asset for the teleconferencing rep. Perseverance counts.

One nonuser had some specific advice for vendors. "Vendors need to promote it with top executives by finding something that will interest them in using it. They need to stimulate use at upper levels with something to provide that gives a competitive edge."

What Would Change Their Minds?

The 22 nonusers interviewed were asked about factors that would encourage them to use teleconferencing as user companies do today. In addition, we asked them what it would take to stimulate this industry to realize the potential so often predicted for it. As might be expected, the responses to the second half of the question were fairly general, but the respondents mentioned four factors repeatedly. First, prices would have to come down for business in general to adopt some forms of teleconferencing. Second, all forms of teleconferencing must be easy to use—user friendly, as the cliche says. Third, teleconferencing would need to be applications oriented. No one is interested in investing a substantial sum in a black box without knowing what lurks beneath the lid and what function it can serve. Finally, the world at large needs more success stories. It remains true that the best means of encouraging new use is to have evidence of existing use.

The interviewees were more specific when asked about factors within their own organizations that would encourage teleconferencing use. The four factors mentioned above were emphasized on a more personal level. Additionally, respondents mentioned ongoing problems. Management, they said, needed to endorse teleconferencing before it could be accepted, and many managers were leery of the technology or fearful that it would deprive them of perks (primarily travel). The main obstacle within the company was attitudinal. "We're high touch, not high tech," said one. "The company just isn't innovative enough," said another. "People need to be educated, they need to be aware of the competitive advantages,'' said a third.

It is interesting to note that these respondents talked about high costs as a primary objection when asked about previous failures in adopting teleconferencing systems. Yet, when asked about the potential for successful introduction of teleconferencing within their own organizations, their primary interest was in overcoming the negative attitudes of management. This corresponds to the observations of teleconferencing users that cost is not the primary factor in the installation and use of a system. It is far more important to sell the concept, the advantages of teleconferencing.

It is worthwhile to compare the comments of nonusers to those of users. The users, for the most part, have installed and maintained systems *despite* tremendous difficulties in finding vendors who can develop and service an appropriate system. Given the obstacles confronting the nonusers and the problems experienced by the seasoned veterans, we may well ask, ''How does anyone ever manage to become a teleconferencing user?''

Life is difficult for the prospective user trying to introduce teleconferencing. Such early users are confronted with many obstacles:

Overcoming negative organizational attitudes

Finding strong teleconferencing advocates

Justifying the cost

Developing appropriate applications

Dealing with uncooperative or overloaded vendors

Vendors can help remove most of these obstacles, and they could completely eliminate the last one. But vendors of teleconferencing have their own views regarding why users do not purchase their products.

VENDORS ON NONUSERS

Teleconferencing vendors are concerned about the large number of nonusers. Users are the key to a vendor's success and profitability; the more users, the better for business. To them, large pools of nonusers conjure images (sometimes inappropriately) of the failure of their technology, of their marketing effort, or of both. We conducted interviews with 12 vendors of a wide range of teleconferencing products and services to assess their feelings about nonusers and their own perceptions of barriers in the teleconferencing marketplace. The vendors represented the following product categories: audio only, audiographic, freeze-frame, audio-bridging services, two-way full-motion video, two-way compressed motion video, and one-way full-motion video (Business TV). Among the group were past and present providers of public-room or public-access two-way full-motion video room services, perhaps the hardest sell in teleconferencing today.

We present in the following pages candid views from these representative industry vendors. Their comments—a mixture of self-criticism, microscopic scrutiny of the marketplace, and reexaminations of users' responses to their marketing efforts—are particularly insightful. We feel they have direct relevance not only to teleconferencing, but to groupware products.

We asked all the vendors to name the two or three most important reasons why there are still so many nonusers of teleconferencing. Their answers cluster around four main sets of factors—three are internal to an organization, the other is external to it. The factor sets are *psychological, technological, organizational* (all internal), and *external marketplace*. Figure 22 shows the framework for their answers graphically.

The internal factors are not mutually exclusive, hence the diagram showing their intersections. We shall first take a close look at the psychological, technological, and organizational factors.

Psychological Factors

The predominant feeling expressed among the vendors is that the *concept* of teleconferencing is not well understood. Teleconferencing is a means of communication, nothing else. When done successfully, its effects may be savings in personnel time, travel dollars, and a host of other benefits, but that is not its function. At the heart of the concept of teleconferencing is the notion that if its users enhance much-needed group communication across geography, they will improve their operational efficiency, and the benefits will follow. These benefits can be of any kind, and they differ across organizations. The labels put on them depend on the particular benefits obtained.

FIGURE 22

Factors Affecting the Use of Teleconferencing

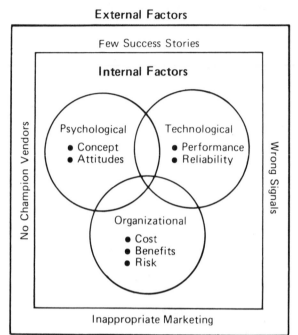

"The problem of concept is very real for potential users," one person stated, "the concept of teleconferencing is still too fuzzy in their minds. Some think of it as a fad that will come and go. It makes for a hard sell." "You cannot sell people something they don't understand," he added. And in one outburst, a vendor insisted, "You want to talk about understanding the concept—we could give away video rooms free and people would not flock to them." This is clearly a cry for more and better education of teleconferencing's potential on the part of everyone, but especially vendors who have the most direct contact with potential users. Vendors must make a connection to concepts that the nonusers can understand. A similar problem, of course, is occurring with groupware products.

One key point, emphasized by many respondents, is that the shift from an emphasis on travel displacement to one on productivity enhancement has been slow. It is beginning now, however, as evidence by an increased emphasis on productivity gains in actual business cases.

The second most prevalent psychological barrier was specific *attitudes* that tended to discourage purchases. "Such attitudes were not necessarily shared by many people, but by significant people who either had signature authority or who could influence sales." The following list gives the most frequently mentioned attitudes by the vendors who were quoting the views of potential clients who had turned them down:

"Our company, and many others, are not culturally prepared to take on teleconferencing in a big way."

"We believe it is still too new and doesn't come naturally or spontaneously for most people."

"We feel it is a behavior change that is likely to take quite a while to get used to."

"We are scared to take the risk, afraid of failure."

Vendors know about this psychological component but seem to view it as an obstacle rather than as an opportunity. Every potential customer has a specific set of conceptual/attitudinal objections to teleconferencing. Vendors should make a deliberate effort to uncover these objections and to address them directly. Many of these objections reflect the customer's reluctance to support anything that may prove to be an expensive and visible failure. Customers need to be assured that the risk is minimal. Many psychological factors tend to be related to technological factors and to a lack of comfort with the technology.

Technological Factors

Lots of potential users are disillusioned when their first exposure to teleconferencing is not positive. Not only must the technology be easy to use, it must work well. It must also be reliable. Reliability of the technology has been rated among the top criteria users want in any system. "Reliability statistics are seen by many users as less than satisfactory and they have complained to vendors. Reliability, that is, percent downtime of any system, is tolerated at about 2%. This industry seems to be averaging closer to 5% . . . its that 5% they remember," said one of our respondents. The consensus of the re-

spondents was that the fewer buttons to push, the greater the acceptance of the technology and its saleability. Here are some of their
thoughts on the technologies of teleconferencing:

Audio vendor: "Teleconferencing users do not wish to learn to
program; they want answers from pushing *few* buttons. Most
equipment calls for pushing too many buttons."

Audiographic equipment vendor: "Teleconferencing technology
outside of speaker-phones is still too experimental. In no way can
we claim it is proven technology."

Satellite videoconferencing vendor: "Frankly, we must admit the
technologies of teleconferencing are still somewhat unreliable—
there are still too many breakdowns or failures that tend to turn
people off. I would guess that 20 percent of users have an unsuc-
cessful first experience—something fails."

Full-motion video equipment vendor: "The problem is not so
much our equipment—it is simply the fact that managers and executives are blasted every day with new technology—some will
suffer. Teleconferencing may be among those that are not of high
priority."

Asked if they thought the lack of standards hindered sales, respondents were split on the issue. About half of the group felt that it
was a major barrier *to international sales* but not a serious handicap
domestically. One-third felt that there was definitely a large pool of
nonusers who are put off by the lack of standards and are playing a
waiting game until a common standard is adopted or some easy
means of interconnectivity is widespread. The remainder felt it was
not a serious issue because the industry was still young and the technologies were changing rapidly.

Technology can be an asset; some users do want to have state-of-
the-art equipment. They do not want state-of-the-art equipment that
is untested, unreliable, or overpriced, however. Justifying a new
black box to management (particularly in a nontechnical organization) can be tricky. The vendor must work to create a positive image
of teleconferencing—a money, time, and effort saver; a money
maker; a strategic tool; a productivity tool. To do so inevitably involves dealing with organizational factors.

Organizational Factors

Costs and benefits are intertwined, especially if justification of teleconferencing systems in an organization is required. Poor cost-benefit analysis by corporations was considered the most important organizational factor vendors faced when trying to sell companies that eventually did not purchase a system. The higher the level of investment involved in a teleconferencing system, the more important such analyses become. Vendors of full-motion video systems say they often cannot get over the cost hurdle in many companies because both transmission and video equipment at today's prices just seem too expensive.

One ad hoc video vendor said he is glad he no longer has to sell two-way full-motion video systems because, "point-to-point is cost prohibitive—management wants to see cost effectiveness. They can see it in ad hoc and dedicated point-to-multipoint networks." One marketing representative of a major manufacturer of teleconferencing equipment had just lost three sales (which he thought were in the bag) when we spoke to him. "The arithmetic did not come out right for us—corporations don't approach teleconferencing in a true cost-benefit analysis mode because they don't understand benefits or do not want to accept them where they cannot quantify them."

The primary benefits of teleconferencing are soft, but systems are often justified in hard dollars. This poses a dilemma to both the vendor trying to sell the product and often to the middle manager putting together the business case for upper management approval. "What's more," a prominent vendor said, "until we get good measurement tools to quantify *productivity,* some companies will not accept our claims that teleconferencing will enhance productivity." Clearly, potential users need to take certain hard-to-quantify benefits on faith or consult with satisfied user companies about the benefits they are currently getting from their use of teleconferencing.

The minimum-of-two rule is another barrier. Because we are dealing with communication across at least two locations, the company needs two of most (if not all) pieces of equipment. The costs add up.

Another organizational factor respondents stressed was the fact that there is an increasing perception in many companies that introducing teleconferencing is a high-risk undertaking. "If it works well, you are a hero; if it busts, you're in big trouble," was one observation. "In fact, I am sure, after two clear-cut examples, that there is some sabotage at work. . . . They justify it poorly, it fails to be approved, so they eliminate the risk." This may smack of paranoia on the part of one vendor, but the same sentiments were expressed at a recent teleconference summit meeting at which many industry leaders were present. They seemed to agree that there is that degree of career risk in some cases.

Within an organization a number of other factors seem to conspire against a smooth sell. For one, "resistance to change is so high that the internal sell within the organization is very hard—even where the person who is doing the business case understands teleconferencing well," complained one person. For another, the internal sell can sometimes go through various layers within the organization and still get nowhere, especially when the idea for teleconferencing comes from people who have little clout or little legitimacy in the company. "They try to sell the idea to the telecom manager, who often does not know what the game is all about. Then he or she tries MIS, who knows even less, and so it goes on."

The organizational factor is probably the most critical of the three internal factors. Unfortunately for the vendor, dealing with the internal factors is not enough. Too many factors outside the organization—problems with the teleconferencing industry itself—handicap sales efforts.

External Factors

Many of the equipment and service providers we talked to believe the marketplace has sent mixed signals to potential users that may have confused these would-be users. Asked what these signals were, they elaborated as follows:

"On the one hand, we have told them for the last few years all these wonderful things about teleconferencing as a rapidly growing market, but there has been no boom—no explosion. On top of that, the negative press has had more effect than the positive press."

"Part of the fault is ours—we hyped it too much. We promised it as travel substitution, now we are making an about turn; potential users are not dumb. They are being cautious, and who can blame them?"

Virtually all the interviewees felt there were not enough success stories to convince potential users that teleconferencing is for real. "There are some, but not enough . . . and what's more, there are lots of successful *uses* but not enough successful *user systems*," was one pertinent observation. As another said, "Success stories! Tell me about them. Where are the big *Fortune* companies who are telling the world this thing is great, you cannot do without it?"

One factor in the external environment that clearly has been responsible for vendors' failures to win potential clients has been inappropriate marketing of teleconferencing products and services. Some of them were among the first to admit this. More than half of those we surveyed admitted the fallacy of the travel-replacement methods of marketing. "We marketed technology, not applications . . . in hindsight we were wrong, but I don't think anyone thought so at the time" is a typical reply.

One vendor who enjoys very good success with his product (which is fixed or portable at the user's convenience) had this to say:

"We as vendors have tried bringing technology willy-nilly into the companies' corporate culture rather than learn how the corporate culture could fit the product. How many of us vendors do our homework on the copmanies we try to sell? Some of us are too small to spend money on staff to do that—that's a big problem."

He added:

"The other thing we've done wrong in marketing is how we give demos. I am now learning after over 300 unit sales in the last two years, that it is best to give a demo, leave the equipment for no more than two weeks—then pull it out. Let them miss it if they've grown to love it, if they haven't used it much by then, they may not be serious. That's my philosophy."

That tactic does not always work, however, as another provider pointed out. "I give them 30 to 60 days risk-free opportunity to test the product, and that has worked extremely well for me."

BREAKING DOWN THE BARRIERS

The vendors interviewed repeated similar answers to the question, "What is needed most to make teleconferencing realize its full potential?" The responses fell into four basic categories:

1. *Education.* The general public does not really know what tele-conferencing is and what it can do. (This belief contradicts the findings in the nonuser interviews—most of the nonusers seemed to understand teleconferencing and its basic uses.) This is a handy excuse for the vendors if they can convince themselves that educating the public is not their task. "Only AT&T is large enough to do that," said one vendor. Nevertheless, several of the vendors thought that education was of prime importance. The nonusers interviewed, conversely, would probably have been somewhat offended at the implication that they "needed education." Some of the more-cynical nonusers might have noted that this conclusion reflected the fact that the vendors do not know their markets.

2. *Corporate culture.* Attitudes of management are often a problem, as nonusers agree. As one vendor said, "The attitude of management needs to change. They are afraid of risky projects tied to their careers that appear to have a high probability of failure and are unwilling to accept teleconferencing benefits on faith."

3. *Publicity.* Success stories and vocal advocates are lacking. This brings up the old paradox—no one wants to drive the bandwagon, but everyone is willing to jump on it. How can a vendor sell teleconferencing to the first group of users when no one will join the first group? "We need big companies saying 'we are using it, we are proud of it, and you should be using it too.'" Granted this would be nice, but no company is going to exert itself in such a manner unless the system—and the vendor—are truly remarkable and there is a clear incentive for telling their story.

4. *Features.* This category is a miscellaneous one encompassing various product changes or enhancements that vendors deem necessary for complete public acceptance. It includes items such as improved product packaging, products integrated into the office system, lower-priced products, more-reliable products, and a larger number of choices for the potential customer.

These responses are hardly surprising but they may be profound. The most interesting aspect about them is that the vendors consistently overlook the importance of their own potential contribution to the solution. Obviously, they know that they could lower the prices or perhaps produce a more-compact unit. But they do not seem to realize that many potential customers are not buying because *no one has sold the product to them*—at least not the way it needs to be sold.

It is somewhat shortsighted to emphasize factors such as education. Vendors who talk about education are reflecting their belief that the *customer* needs to change. The customer is not going to change, certainly not because the vendor wants a change to occur. The vendor has to accept as a *given* the realization that customers, in all probability, are not going to be interested in educating themselves. Vendors must look to factors over which they have control— their own promotional and sales efforts. Vendors also need to take a hard look at their most prominent failures, major organizations who tried teleconferencing and then backed away.

LESSONS FOR GROUPWARE

Teleconferencing implementation can fail for many reasons. The interview results summarized earlier in this chapter provide a taste for these reasons. In addition, we have done case studies of specific situations in which teleconferencing has failed. Table 18 lists 21 fail-

Table 18   FAILURE FACTORS IN TELECONFERENCING

1. Did not perform accurate needs assessment
2. System not promoted internally
3. Technology unsuited to organizational culture
4. Performed poor cost-benefit analysis
5. Wrong timing
6. Overemphasized travel substitution
7. No department willing to champion the cause
8. Technology did not match perceived application
9. No feeling of "ownership" of the system
10. No top-down endorsement
11. Too much comparison to face-to-face meetings
12. System not easily accessible to potential users
13. Concept not well understood
14. System was too project specific—a limited pool of users
15. Poor facilitation—no commitment to the system, little training
16. Technology not easy to use
17. Little or no emphasis on training users
18. Senior management not involved until too late
19. System resisted for political reasons
20. Overseas management (where important) not made sufficiently involved
21. Wrong first user groups

ure factors that we have identified from years of analyzing both successes and failures. The factors are not ranked in any order. They are all important. Any one of them at any time could have carried sufficient weight to inhibit system use or discourage teleconferencing in the organization.

A lot can be learned from these factors as the use of groupware is considered. Some factors are technology related (for example, ease of use). Others are organizational (for example, poor facilitation, little emphasis on training) and clearly are in the purview of the user company. And some are conceptual, such as the recurring "what is it?" problem.

These failure factors should be viewed as vivid warnings for both users and vendors of groupware. They represent a balance to the success stories that introduced this section. There is no need to remake these old mistakes, provided that the traps are recognized and ways around the traps are developed. Just as the teleconferencing vendors have learned (some are still learning), there are psychological, technological, and organizational factors to consider, and the business climate will not necessarily be working in favor of groupware efforts. Learning from the successes and failures of teleconferencing can increase greatly the probabilites of groupware success.

APPENDIX B

Silicon Valley Surprises

Experience with markets for new information technologies has yielded at least one underlying lesson: prepare to be surprised. Thus, it seems appropriate to try to anticipate surprises and perhaps bet on them or try to influence them. Of particular interest is whether there are technological developments that could change the outlook for groupware by enhancing it, making it easier, making it more difficult, or making it irrelevant in some way. These developments are important to monitor, because a slow-growing market could change quickly if certain surprises occurred.

These surprises are developments in technology, applications, products, or industry structure that could realistically (a probability of between 10 and 25 percent) take place *in the next five years* that would affect the emergence of groupware. We refer to them as *Silicon Valley Surprises,* but we have certainly been looking beyond Northern California.

The surprises have been identified through workshops at IFTF and a follow-up process. The focus of the workshops was on generating ideas regarding certain changes in technology, applications, products, or industry structure that might emerge from technology companies in the next five years and that could change the outlook for communication through computers. The primary workshop generated approximately 60 candidates. The follow-up process provided more details about how the development could affect groupware. We now present eight of these ideas that could have a large effect on the market, and we hope they will stimulate further creative thinking by readers about surprises that could alter the prospects of groupware.

179

INTEROPERABILITY WORKS, QUICKLY

Surprise

Many efforts are under way to resolve the main incompatibilities among computers that prevent easy communication and frustrate users. The most common approach is to issue standards. Mark Stefik of Xerox PARC, in his work on AI as a knowledge medium, has advanced the notion of *interoperability*.[1] He holds that although standards are essential at certain levels, they can only go so far toward mediating the differences between systems. As systems become more complex, the number of standards needed to reconcile them becomes unmanageable. Worse, the standards cannot really handle the complexity. The surprise, then, is that systems develop quickly (probably making heavy use of AI techniques) to resolve these incompatibilities.

Arguments For

There is a good deal of work going on in many areas today to produce such systems, and standards efforts are encouraging. The simple advantages, such as no more worrying about getting the speed and protocol settings right on the modem or about the correct format for a spreadsheet exchange, are easy to see. But it is the creation of AI communication "agents" that offers the exciting potential. These agents would get the message across as effectively as possible, no matter how incompatible the systems. As with human beings, the message may be incomplete when the cultural differences are large. But for most applications, the message would get through.

Arguments Against

These systems are just plain difficult to construct. Partial solutions are constantly entering the market, satisfying the immediate communication needs of users and further complicating the path for a black box to solve greater communication incompatibilities. The successful black box is not yet visible on the horizon. Meanwhile, those users who really need to communicate will find a way.

Implications

It is certain that something like interoperability will be built into systems; the questions concern timing and how good such systems will be. The sooner something like interoperability is built into most systems as a standard feature, the sooner marketers can set to work showing users how simple and fast it is to communicate through computers. Until then, it will remain neither fast nor simple. Should interoperability occur quickly, even on a limited scale, one of the major barriers to group communication through computers would be removed. Our judgment is that powerful systems will not be common on the market for at least four years, unless there is a surprise. . . .

PUBLIC KEY ENCRYPTION IS WIDELY IMPLEMENTED

Surprise

Public key encryption (PKE) permits users on a system to send encrypted messages among themselves without prior agreement. Conventional encryption systems are rather cumbersome and difficult to use, requiring both the sender and receiver to agree on a key. With PKE, each user has a public password and a private password. Senders encrypt with the receiver's public password; the receiver's private password is the only way to decrypt the message.

Arguments For

PKE algorithms have additional properties that make them quite attractive for business communications. Different sequences of encryption and decryption with users' public and private passwords yield properties that resemble signatures, time stamps, meeting quorums, locks, and other essentials of business.

Arguments Against

Most PKE algorithms rely on number theoretic properties that are too computation-intensive for today's personal computers. Further, any encryption is more cumbersome than none at all. Designers of other secure systems have found that users often do not use (and sometimes actively circumvent) security features. Also, some people in the cryptography community feel that PKE algorithms may be inherently vulnerable to a number of theoretic attacks.

Implications

Many current systems for electronic mail and other forms of computer communications warn against using them for confidential information. By making encrypted communication easier, PKE (or some other form of powerful security aid) can open groupware for many new applications. Users who stay away from electronic mail because of security or privacy worries, however, must trust the systems enough to use them. It is not even clear that PKE will be perceived as secure by the users.

RADIO LANs REPLACE WIRE

Surprise

A common barrier to the implementation of LANs in the office setting is the high cost of installing new wiring. Retrofits in older buildings that do not have suspended ceilings or easily accessible walls are particularly difficult. One technology that could reduce costs considerably is a radio (that is, "wireless") LAN; in principle, it is technologically feasible.

Argument For

The advantages are inexpensive installation and total flexibility. The network could grow node by node. No new wiring would be needed, nor would the building need to be prewired. Similarly, when the configuration of the network changed, either physically or logically, no wiring changes would be required. Given sufficient bandwidth, such as system could also replace existing office telephone systems.

Argument Against

One substantial barrier to radio LANs is the crowding of the electromagnetic spectrum, both in regulation and in reality. It is not clear that LAN makers could get regulatory permission to use the FM frequency band (though below a certain power, no FCC license is needed). Even if they could, they would probably be operating at frequencies similar to other devices in the office, risking interference. Also, in business concerned with data security, the prospect of having business information "on the air" would not be acceptable.

Implications

Radio LANs at a low price could mean a much faster takeoff of LAN installation. With appropriate software, more LANs mean more use of groupware.

VIDEOBASES AND AUDIOBASES BECOME PRACTICAL

Surprise

There is a large disparity between how we handle text and how we handle images and audio. Text handling has a model paper file systems in which we index, store, retrieve, combine, and catalog information. The systems of titles, numbers, and other indices make it easy to get to a piece of information. Databases composed of video and audio material are not yet widely used. This candidate surprise is that a practical commercial system for cataloging, indexing, and processing these signals is developed and catches on within the next five years.

Arguments For

The use of video and audio in all parts of business and society is increasing. Video has received the lion's share of recent attention, with applications on videotape, videodisk, photo bases on personal computers, and presentation aids. But the real payoff may be in audiobases. One implication of our enthusiasm for the prospects of voice mail is that some method of handling the volume of messages will be needed—a method to discard ephemeral messages and to store and catalog permanent ones.

Arguments Against

It is not yet clear that enough significant transactions will take place by voice mail to warrant keeping many messages. The tendency (as with phone calls and face-to-face meetings) is to back up any important exchange with a paper memo. There are also major technical problems to be overcome before such systems become practical.

Implications

Audiobases have the potential, with proper search tools, to extend the range of communications that take place through electronic systems. One important feature will be integration with other forms of document storage. Thus, a user seeking all communications on a certain issue would be presented a list of paper, electronic text, audio, and perhaps video documents.

INTELLIGENT TEXT PROCESSING BECOMES PRACTICAL

Surprise

Once a business person makes extensive use of a PC, the problem of information management becomes severe. None of the functions that clerical and secretarial staff perform today—filing, abstracting, selecting, filtering junk mail—are performed automatically on computer systems. Intelligent text processing applies principles of AI to accomplish these jobs. This area of research is already important, and a few interesting products have appeared. The surprise would be the rapid practical development of these capabilities with five years.

Arguments For

Many of the pieces of the puzzle are in place today. File utilities are available that take care of some of the problems of file management. Experimental systems read all the news on a wire service and construct a custom newspaper for the user. Spelling checkers reduce the burden of proofreading. Desktop publishing systems provide high-quality print output. It would seem that "all" that must be done is to integrate these pieces.

Arguments Against

That task of integration is much more difficult than may be expected. It is difficult enough (interoperability notwithstanding) to make a single file transfer from one word processor to another. These systems must face the trade-off between standardization and flexibility. The results from AI experiments to date are not as promising with tasks that require flexibility and multiple objectives as they are with discrete tasks.

Implications

Intelligent text processing is most likely to be implemented in user organizations that can impose some standards on the format of documents that they produce. We expect major gains in the next five years within innovative user organizations. In those organizations, there will be gains in user friendliness and the utility of their systems. In others, attempts at intelligent text processing are likely to be chaotic. Still, if they succeed, group effectiveness would be increased greatly.

One interesting application could be to identify affinity and interest groups electronically. An "electronic grapevine" could develop that would detect and put people with shared interests in touch. Such a system, of course, could also be used for less-innocent purposes.

COLLABORATIVE SYSTEMS BECOME FRIENDLY *AND* POWERFUL

Surprise

The hardware that services people communicating through computers has many complex functions. Most of the shared workspaces and collaborative systems require sophisticated users and operators.

Although each of the operations the systems perform has a natural analogy in human interaction (yield the floor, interrupt, share an image, substantiate an argument), the structures established in today's systems are complicated and difficult to use.

It is still too early in the life and development of these systems to expect congeniality to be achieved, but one development that could make these products acceptable and interesting to an audience of noncomputer science Ph.D.'s would be interfaces that replicate the ways we communicate. At the same time, collaborative systems should also provide people the power to increase their group performance beyond what is possible with current tools.

Arguments For

Several R&D laboratories have major efforts under way to understand the human aspects of using collaborative systems. Both hardware and software solutions are being developed, evaluated, and refined. Systems in laboratories today could be on the market in a few years, given signals that there would be a demand.

Arguments Against

The conventions that we use in human interaction are so complex and subtle that no software (barring an AI breakthrough) can really replicate them without drastic oversimplification. Too much simplification would make the interactions so artificial as to make them unappealing to most users. Also, lack of user friendliness is only one of the reasons that there is not yet a large market for collaborative systems. It is not clear that even friendly systems would sell well, because there is not an orientation among users toward collaborative work.

Implications

Collaborative systems would become accessible to nontechnical user groups. Thus, a major barrier to people communicating through computers would be eliminated. Many of these user interface techniques would probably be applicable to other types of systems as well, so that a whole host of adaptive, congenial applications would be developed.

AN EFFECTIVE VOICEWRITER IS DEVELOPED

Surprise

One technological development that would make computers accessible to a wider range of users is voicewriter: a machine that translates free-form spoken language into computer text. Among the important parameters are whether it is speaker dependent or speaker independent, the amount of time required in "training" it to recognize a voice, and the error rate.

Arguments For

A great many developments have been made in recent years in the right direction. Speaker-dependent machines with a limited vocabulary are now available as add-on boards for personal computers. Speaker-independent machines with tiny vocabularies are also available. Promising voicewriters already have been announced.

Arguments Against

The error rates on current large-vocabulary machines are still unacceptably high. Remember that 95 percent accuracy means that 1 in 20 words is wrongly transcribed. It may be that a software breakthrough (rather than an incremental increase in speed or power) is needed to make a very functional voicewriter. Predicting the timing of such breakthroughs is notoriously difficult.

Implications

A user interface that incorporates some speech understanding (interpretation) along with transcription opens the market for computers and for communication through computers to a whole new group of users. Many who would not consider a computer because they could not or would not use a keyboard would have a much easier access to computing.

USERS DEMAND SYSTEMS FOR COLLABORATIVE WORK

Surprise

A consensus develops among users that communication through computers is a good thing. In particular, companies with dispersed work groups see computer communication as a necessity. Ultimately, all "good" companies use these tools. This consensus could be stimulated by a business fad (à la Japanese management styles or the book *In Search of Excellence*) or a provocative new product (à la Visicalc, Lotus 1-2-3, or the IBM PC).

Arguments For

Many companies with a reputation for leadership are already supporting their groups with computers. For some, the competitive advantage is real and has been noticed. Articles on communication through computers have appeared in the *Harvard Business Review, Business Week,* and *Fortune,* emphasizing the need for such systems to gain a competitive advantage. Silicon Valley companies are expressing strong interest in group-oriented products.

Arguments Against

The inertia of companies and their resistance to changing established communication patterns can never be overestimated. There is a strong "show me" contingent, and many of these resident skeptics are responsible for making purchasing decisions. No group application is yet on the horizon.

Implications

Development of a user consensus would more fundamentally change our main forecast than any other surprise. None of the supply-side developments—an increase in capabilities, more congeniality, lower prices—could have an effect as profound as a strong surge in demand.

Notes

CHAPTER 1

1. Murray Turoff, "Delphi Conferencing: Computer-Based Conferencing with Anonymity," *Technological Forecasting and Social Change,* 1972, Volume 3, pp. 159-204.

2. For a summary of Jacques Vallee's views on this work and his explorations of commercial systems, see Jacques Vallee, *Computer Message Systems,* New York: McGraw-Hill, 1984. See also Robert Johansen and R. De Grasse, "Computer-Based Teleconferencing: Effects on Working Patterns," *Journal of Communication,* Summer 1979.

3. See S.R. Hiltz and M. Turoff, *The Network Nation-Human Communication via Computer,* Reading, MA: Addison-Wesley, 1978.

4. Douglas C. Engelbart, "A Conceptual Framework for the Augmentation of Man's Intellect," in Paul W. Howerton and David C. Weeks, *Vistas in Information Handling,* Volume 1, Washington, DC: Spartan Books, 1963, pp. 1-29.

5. Douglas C. Engelbart, Richard W. Watson, and James C. Norton, "The Augmented Knowledge Workshop," in *AFIPS Conference Proceedings,* Volume 42, National Computer Conference and Exposition, June 4-8, 1973, New York City, Montvale, NJ: AFIPS Press.

6. *Proceedings of the Conference on Computer-Supported Cooperative Work,* December 3-5, 1986.

7. *Proceedings from Symposium on Technological Support for Work Group Collaboration,* Center for Research on Information Systems, Graduate School of Business, New York University, May 21-22, 1987.

8. Peter Nulty, "Pushed Out at 45—Now What?," *Fortune,* March 2, 1987, p. 26.

9. Quoted in *The Wall Street Journal,* October 13, 1987.

10. "Behind the Brands at P&G: An Interview with John Smale," *Harvard Business Review,* November-December 1985, pp. 78-90.

11. Milton Pierce, "25 Lessons from the Japanese," *New Management,* Volume 5, Number 2, Fall 1987, pp. 23-31.

12. Louis S. Richman, "Software Catches the Team Spirit," *Fortune,* June 8, 1987.

CHAPTER 2

1. Peter G.W. Keen and Michael S. Scott Morton, *Decision Support Systems,* Reading, MA: Addison-Wesley, 1978.

2. Kenneth L. Kraemer and John Leslie King, "Computer-Based Systems for Co-operative Work and Group Decisionmaking: Status of Use and Problems in Development," in *Proceedings of the Conference on Computer-Supported Co-operative Work,* December 3–5, 1986, pp. 353–375. Another excellent summary of GDSS work is contained in Paul Gray, "Group Decision Support Systems," in *Decision Support Systems: A Decade in Perspective,* E. R. McLean and H. G. Sol (eds.), New York: Elsevier Science Publishers (North-Holland), 1986.

3. For an example of research on group calendaring, see Irene Greif and Sunil Sarin, "Data Sharing in Group Work," in Proceedings of the Conference on Computer-Supported Cooperative Work, op. cit., pp. 175–183. Reprinted in *ACM Transactions on Office Information Systems,* April 1987.

4. For an overview of four current products, see Richard Dalton, "Group-Writing Tools: Four That Connect," *Information Week,* March 9, 1987. We have not listed names here, because it is too early to predict which ones will survive.

5. For a basic description of Colab, see Mark Stefik, Gregg Foster, Daniel G. Bobrow, Kenneth Kahn, Stan Lanning, and Lucy Suchman, "Beyond the Chalkboard," *Communications of the ACM,* January 1987. Colab also in-cludes functions involved in nine other scenarios introduced in this paper.

6. Several of the commercial and research efforts are described in Kraemer and King, op. cit. Also, ICL has a system called The Pod, which is specially designed for group decision support and is designed in modular units.

7. The early problems of implementing WYSIWIS are described in M. Stefik, D.G. Bobrow, G. Foster, S. Lanning, and D. Tatar, "WYSIWIS Revised: Early Experiences with Multiuser Interfaces," *ACM Transactions on Office Informa-tion Systems,* Volume 5, Number 2, April 1987, pp. 147–167.

8. For a broad vision of what computer conferencing might do, see Murray Turoff and Roxanne Hiltz, *The Network Nation,* op. cit., Chapter 1. For a comparison of early social evaluations of computer conferencing, both pro and con, see Robert Johansen, Jacques Vallee, and Kathleen Vian, *Electronic Meetings,* Reading, MA: Addison-Wesley, 1979.

9. For a basic description of this work, see Thomas W. Malone, Kenneth R. Grant, Franklyn A. Turbak, Stephen A. Brobst, and Michael D. Cohen, "Intel-ligent Information Sharing Systems," *Communications of the ACM,* May 1987, Volume 30, Number 5, pp. 390–402. The "Information Lens" is a research environment that cuts across the 17 scenarios identified in this paper; it is di-rectly relevant to 12 of the 17 scenarios.

10. A summary of the approach embodied in the Coordinator is contained in Fer-nando Flores and Chauncey Bell, "A New Understanding of Managerial Work Improves System Design," *Computer Technology Review,* Fall 1984. For more detail on the conceptual underpinnings, see Terry Winograd and Fernando Flores, *Understanding Computers and Cognition,* Norwood, NJ: Ablex, 1986.

11. For a concise summary of NoteCards, see Frank G. Halasy, Thomas P. Moran, and Randall H. Trigg, "NoteCards in a Nutshell," Xerox Palo Alto Research Center, Submitted to CHI+GI 1987, Toronto, Canada, April 5–9, 1987.

12. Gordon B. Thompson, "An Assessment Methodology for Evaluating Commu-

nications Innovations," *IEEE Transactions on Communications,* Volume COM-23, Number 10, October 1975, p. 1048.

13. For a summary of the SCL activities, see G.O. Goodman and M.J. Abel, "Communication and Collaboration: Facilitating Cooperative Work Through Communications," *Office Technology and People,* Volume 3, Number 2, August 1987, pp. 129–146.

14. The now classic statement of Engelbart's vision is contained in D.C. Engelbart, "A Conceptual Framework for the Augmentation of Man's Intellect," op. cit., Chapter 1.

15. The notion of a nonhuman participant in electronic meetings is described in some detail in scenarios included in Robert Johansen, *Teleconferencing and Beyond,* New York: McGraw-Hill, 1984, pp. 131–165.

16. See Mark Stefik, "The Next Knowledge Medium," *AI Magazine,* Volume 7, Number 1, Spring 1986.

17. The categorization scheme in Table 4 was stimulated by an excellent article analyzing groupware from a group decision support systems point of view. See Gerardine DeSanctis and R. Brent Gallup, "A Foundation for the Study of Group Decision Support Systems," *Management Science,* Volume 33, No. 5, May 1987.

CHAPTER 4

1. This quote came from a senior corporate strategist at a major computer manufacturer that is supporting upstream R&D on computer-supported groups.

2. For a description of some of these problems, see Irene Greif and Sunil Sarin, "Data Sharing in Group Work," op. cit., Chapter 2.

CHAPTER 5

1. As best we can determine, the term *softer software* was first used by Microsoft President Bill Gates.

2. Avron Barr and Edward A. Feigenbaum, "The Handbook of Artificial Intelligence," Volume 1, p. 3, Los Altos, CA: William Kaufman, 1981.

3. Ted Nelson, *Computer Lib/Dream Machines.* Tempus Books/Microsoft Press, 1987.

4. Vannevar Bush, "As We May Think," *Atlantic Monthly,* July 1945, pp. 101–108.

5. The best overview of hypertext we have seen is Jeff Conklin, "Hypertext: An Introduction and Survey," *IEEE Computer,* September 1987, pp. 17–42.

6. See Danny Goodman, *The Complete Hypercard Handbook,* New York: Bantam Books, 1987.

7. See M. Stefik et al., "WYSIWIS Revised . . . " op. cit., Chapter 2.

8. See Mark Stefik, "The Next Knowledge Medium," op. cit., Chapter 2.

9. See Gregg Foster and Mark Stefik, "Cognoter, Theory and Practice in a Collaborative Tool," *Proceedings of the Conference on Computer-Supported Cooperative Work,* December 3–5, 1986, pp. 7–15.

CHAPTER 7

1. A number of methodologies are relevant here, each of which is applicable to both office systems and planning in other areas of organizational change. We have been particularly impressed with work on critical success factors (J. F. Rockart, "Chief Executives Define Their Own Data Needs," *Harvard Business Review,* March-April 1979, p. 81; and C. V. Bullen and J. F. Rockart, "A Primer on Critical Success Factors," Sloan School of Management, MIT, CISR WP no. 69, June 1981); and the Office Analysis Methodology (M. Sirbu, S. Schoichet, J. S. Kunin, M. Hammer, and J. Sutherland, "OAM: An Office Analysis Methodology," *Proceedings of the Office Automation Conference,* Arlington, VA: American Federation of Information Processing Press, April 1982). The work by Tapscott is also very useful (D. Tapscott, *Office Automation: A User-Driven Method,* New York: Plenum, 1982), as is that of Bair (Ronald J. Uhlig, D. J. Farber, and J. H. Bair, *The Office of the Future,* New York: North Holland, 1979). See also Robert Johansen and Ellen Baker, "User Needs Workshops: A New Approach to Anticipating User Needs for Advanced Office Systems," *Office: Technology and People,* Volume 2 (1984), pp. 103–119.

APPENDIX B

1. Mark Stefik, "The Next Knowledge Medium," op. cit., Chapter 2.

Bibliography

Adamsak, Phil, "Weyerhaueser Rolls On With CIM," *Information Week,* September 21, 1987, pp. 49–51.

Austin, Noel C., "A Management Support Environment," *ICL Technical Journal,* November 1986.

Bair, James H., "Communication in the Office of the Future: Where the Real Pay-Off May Be," *Business Communications Review,* Volume 9, Number 1, January–February 1979.

Bair, James H., "The Need for Collaboration Tools in Offices," Office Automation Conference, 1985 Digest.

Barr, Avron, and Edward A. Feigenbaum, *The Handbook of Artificial Intelligence,* Volume 1, p. 3, Los Altos, CA: William Kaufman, 1981.

Bullen, C.V., and J.F. Rockart, "A Primer on Critical Success Factors," Sloan School of Management, MIT, CISR WP Number 69, June 1981.

Bush, Vannevar, "As We May Think," *Atlantic Monthly,* July 1945, pp. 101–108.

Conklin, Jeff, "Hypertext: An Introduction and Survey," *IEEE Computer,* September 1987, pp. 17–42.

Dalton, Richard, "Group-Writing Tools: Four That Connect," *Information Week,* March 9, 1987, pp. 62–65.

DeSanctis, Gerardine, and Brent Gallupe, "Group Decision Support Systems: A New Frontier," Database, ACM SIGBDP *Bulletin,* Winter 1985, pp. 3–10.

DeSanctis, Gerardine, and R. Brent Gallupe, "A Foundation for the Study of Group Decision Support Systems," *Management Science,* Volume 33, Number 5, May 1987.

DeKoven, Bernard, *Power Meetings,* Palo Alto, CA: C-EM, 1986.

Ellis, Clarence A., "An Office Information System Based upon Migrating Processes," in *Office Information Systems,* N. Naffah, editor, Amsterdam: Elsevier Science Publishers, North Holland, 1982, pp. 3–6.

Engelbart, Douglas C., "A Conceptual Framework for the Augmentation of Man's Intellect," in Paul W. Howerton and David C. Weeks, editors, *Vistas in Information Handling,* Volume 1, Washington, DC: Spartan Books, 1963, pp. 1–29.

Engelbart, Douglas C., Richard W. Watson, and James C. Norton, "The Augmented Knowledge Workshop," in *AFIPS Conference Proceedings,* Volume 42, National Computer Conference and Exposition, June 4–8, 1973, New York City. Montvale, NJ: AFIPS Press.

Eveland, J.D., and T.K. Bikson, "Evolving Electronic Communication Networks: An Empirical Assessment," *Office: Technology and People,* Volume 3, Number 2, August 1987, pp. 103–128.

Feinstein, Debra, "Colab: Toward a Meeting of Minds," *Benchmark,* Fall 1987, pp. 12–14.

Flores, Fernando, and Chauncey Bell, "A New Understanding of Managerial Work Improves System Design," *Computer Technology Review,* Fall 1984, pp. 179–183.

Foster, Gregg, "Collaborative Systems and Multi-user Interfaces," Ph.D. dissertation, University of California, Berkeley, 1986.

Foster, Gregg, and Mark Stefik, "Cognoter, Theory and Practice in a Collaborative Tool," In *Proceedings of the Conference on Computer-Supported Cooperative Work,* New York: ACM, December 3–5, 1986, pp. 7–15.

Gladstein, Deborah L., "Groups in Context: A Model of Task Group Effectiveness," *Administrative Science Quarterly,* Volume 29, 1984, pp. 499–517.

Goodman, Danny, *The Complete Hypercard Handbook,* New York: Bantam Books, 1987.

Goodman, G.O., and M.J. Abel, "Communication and Collaboration: Facilitating Cooperative Work Through Communications," *Office Technology and People,* Volume 3, Number 2, August 1987, pp. 129–146.

Gray, Paul, "Group Decision Support Systems," in *Decision Support Systems: A Decade in Perspective,* E.R. McLean and H.G. Sol, editors, Amsterdam: Elsevier Science Publishers, North-Holland, 1986.

Greif, Irene, and Sunil Sarin, "Data Sharing in Group Work," in *Proceedings of the Conference on Computer-Supported Cooperative Work,* op. cit., pp. 175–183.

Greif, Irene, and Sunil Sarin, "Data Sharing in Group Work," *ACM, Transactions on Office Information Systems,* Volume 5, Number 2, April 1987, pp. 187–211.

Halasy, Frank G., Thomas P. Moran, and Randall H. Trigg, "NoteCards in a Nutshell," Xerox Palo Alto Research Center, CHI '87 Conference, Toronto, Canada, April 5–9, 1987.

Hardaker, Maurice, and Bryan K. Ward, "Getting Things Done," *Harvard Business Review,* November–December 1987, pp. 112–119.

Helmer, Olaf, "Toward the Automation of Delphi," internal technical memorandum, Institute for the Future, Menlo Park, CA, 1970.

Hiltz, S.R., and M. Turoff, *The Network Nation—Human Communication via Computer,* Reading, MA: Addison-Wesley, 1978.

Hiltz, Starr Roxanne, *Online Communities: A Case Study of the Office of the Future,* Norwood, NJ: Ablex Press, 1984.

Huber, George P., "Issues in the Design of Group Decision Support Systems," *MIS Quarterly,* September 1984, pp. 195–204.

Huber, George P., "The Nature and Design of Post-Industrial Organization," *Management Science,* Volume 30, Number 8, August 1984, pp. 928–951.

Huber, George P., "Issues in the Design of Group Decision Support Systems," *MIS Quarterly,* September 1984.

Huber, George P., "Group Decision Support Systems as Aids in the Use of Structured Group Management Techniques," in *DSS-82,* Gary Dickson, editor, Second International Conference on Decision Support Systems Transactions, San Francisco, CA, 1982, pp. 96–108.

Huber, George P., and Reuben R. McDaniel, "The Decision-Making Paradigm of Organizational Design," *Management Science,* Volume 32, Number 5, May 1986.

Johansen, R., and R. De Grasse, "Computer-Based Teleconferencing: Effects on Working Patterns," *Journal of Communication,* Summer 1979.

Johansen, Robert, *Teleconferencing and Beyond,* New York: McGraw-Hill, 1984, pp. 131–165.

Johansen, Robert, and Ellen Baker, "User Needs Workshops: A New Approach to

Anticipating User Needs for Advanced Office Systems," *Office: Technology and People,* Volume 2, Number 2, November 1983, pp. 103–119.

Johansen, Robert, Jacques Vallee, and Kathleen Vian, *Electronic Meetings,* Reading, MA: Addison-Wesley, 1979.

Johnson, Bonnie McDaniel, and Ronald E. Rice, *Managing Organization Innovation,* New York: Columbia University Press, 1987.

Johnson-Lenz, P., and T. Johnson-Lenz, "Groupware: the Emerging Art of Orchestrating Collective Intelligence," presented at the 1st Global Conference on the Future, Toronto, Canada, 1980.

Keen, Peter G.W., and Michael S. Scott Morton, *Decision Support Systems,* Reading, MA: Addison-Wesley, 1978.

Kerr, Elaine, and Starr Roxanne Hiltz, *Computer-Mediated Communication Systems,* New York: Academic Press, 1982.

Kraemer, Kenneth L., and John Leslie King, "Computer-Based Systems for Cooperative Work and Group Decisionmaking: Status of Use and Problems in Development," in *Proceedings of the Conference on Computer-Supported Cooperative Work,* op. cit., pp. 353–375.

Linstone, Harold, and Murray Turoff, *The Delphi Method: Techniques and Applications,* Reading, MA: Addison-Welsey, 1975.

Lowe, David, "Cooperative Structuring of Information: The Representation of Reasoning and Debate," *Journal of Man-Machine Studies,* Volume 23, Number 1, July 1985, pp. 97–111.

Malone, Thomas W., Kenneth R. Grant, Franklyn A. Turbak, Stephen A. Brobst, and Michael D. Cohen, "Intelligent Information Sharing Systems," *Communications of the ACM,* May 1987, Volume 30, Number 5, pp. 390–402. The "Information Lens" is a research environment that cuts across the 17 scenarios identified in this paper; it is directly relevant to 12 of the 17 scenarios.

Meyrowitz, Norman, "Intermedia: The Architecture and Construction of an Object-Oriented Hypermedia System and Applications Framework," in OOPSLA '86 *Conference Proceedings,* Portland, OR, September 1986, pp. 186–201.

Nelson, Theodore, *Dream Machines and Computer Lib,* Chicago: Hugo's Book Service, 1974.

Nulty, Peter, "Pushed Out at 45—Now What?," *Fortune,* March 2, 1987, p. 26.

Nunamaker, Jr., Jay F., Lynda M. Applegate, and Benn R. Konsynski, "Facilitating Group Creativity with GDSS," *Journal of Management Information Systems,* Volume 3, Number 4, Spring 1987, pp. 5–19.

Olson, Margrethe, "Computer-Supported Cooperative Work," *Office: Technology and People,* Volume 3, Number 2, August 1987, pp. 77–81.

Pierce, Milton, "25 Lessons from the Japanese," *New Management,* Volume 5, Number 2, Fall 1987, pp. 23–31.

Proceedings CSCW '85, Conference on Computer-Supported Cooperative Work, December 3–5, 1986, Austin, Texas.

Proceedings of the Conference on Computer-Supported Cooperative Work, New York, Association for Computer Machinery, December 3–5, 1986.

Proceedings from Symposium on Technological Support for Work Group Collaboration, Center for Research on Information Systems, Graduate School of Business, New York University, May 21–22, 1987.

Rice, Ronald, and Associates, *The New Media,* Beverly Hills, CA: Sage, 1984.

Richman, Louis S., "Software Catches the Team Spirit," *Fortune,* June 8, 1987, pp. 125–133

Rockart, J.F., "Chief Executives Define Their Own Data Needs," *Harvard Business Review,* March–April 1979, p. 81.

Seward, Robert Richard, "The Support of Managerial Groups—A New Development," Master's Thesis, University of Lancaster, England, 1987.

Sirbu, M., S. Schoichet, J.S. Kunin, M. Hammer, and J. Sutherland, Office Analysis Methodology, "OAM: An Office Analysis Methodology," *Proceedings of the Office Automation Conference,* Arlington, VA: American Federation of Information Processing Press, April 1982.

Smale, John, "Behind the Brands at P&G: An Interview with John Smale," *Harvard Business Review,* November–December 1985, pp. 78–90.

Sproull, Lee, and Sara Kiesler, "Reducing Social Contest Cues: Electronic Mail in Organizational Communication," *Management Science,* Volume 32, Number 11, 1986, pp. 1492–1512.

Stefik, M., D.G. Bobrow, G. Foster, S. Lanning, and D. Tatar, "WYSIWIS Revised: Early Experiences with Multiuser Interfaces," *ACM Transactions on Office Information Systems,* Volume 5, Number 2, April 1987, pp. 147–167.

Stefik, M., G. Foster, D. Bobrow, K. Kahn, S. Lanning, and L. Suchman, "Beyond the Chalkboard: Computer Support for Collaboration and Problem Solving in Meetings," *Communications of the ACM,* Volume 30, Number 1, January 1987, pp. 32–47.

Stefik, Mark, "The Next Knowledge Medium," *AI Magazine,* Volume 7, Number 1, Spring 1986, pp. 34–46.

Steinfield, Charles W., "Computer-Mediated Communication in an Organizational Setting: Explaining Task-Related and Socioemotional Uses," *Communication Yearbook 9.* Beverly Hills, CA: Sage, 1986.

Strassman, Paul A., *Information Payoff: The Transformation of Work in the Electronic Age,* New York: The Free Press, 1985.

Suchman, Lucy A., and Randall H. Trigg, "A Framework for Studying Research Collaboration," Proceedings of the Conference on Computer Supported Cooperative Work, op. cit., pp. 227–229.

Tapscott, D., *Office Automation: A User-Driven Method,* New York: Plenum, 1982.

Tapscott, Donald, and Jonathan Chevreau, "Farewell to Standalones—and Welcome to Work Groups," *Management Technology,* March 1985, pp. 48–49.

Technological Support for Work Group Collaboration, 1987 NYU Symposium, May 21–22, New York City, Center for Research on Information Systems, New York University.

Thompson, Gordon B., "An Assessment Methodology for Evaluating Communications Innovations," *IEEE Transactions on Communications,* Volume COM-23, Number 10, October 1975, p. 1048.

Trigg, Randall H., Lucy A. Suchman, and Frank G. Halasz, "Supporting Collaboration in Notecards," *Proceedings of the Conference on Computer Supported Cooperative Work,* op. cit., pp. 153–163.

Trigg, Randall H., and Mark Weiser, "TEXTNET: A Network-Based Approach to Text Handling," *ACM Transactions on Office Information Systems,* Volume 4, Number 1, January 1986, pp. 1–23.

Turoff, Murray, "Delphi Conferencing: Computer-Based Conferencing with Anonymity," *Technological Forecasting and Social Change,* 1972, Volume 3, pp. 159–204.

Uhlig, Ronald J., D.J. Farber, and J.H. Bair, *The Office of the Future,* New York: North Holland, 1979.

Vallee, Jacques, *Computer Message Systems,* New York: McGraw-Hill, 1984.

Vallee, Jacques, *The Network Revolution: Confessions of a Computer Scientist,* Berkeley, CA: And/Or Press, Inc., 1982.

Winograd, Terry, and Fernando Flores, *Understanding Computers and Cognition,* Norwood, NJ: Ablex, 1986.

Index